a soul's journey

One woman's journey of healing and surrendering to her gift as a medium

A BOOK ON INSPIRATION, SPIRITUAL HEALING, & PERSONAL GROWTH

MARNIE HILL

Suite 300 - 990 Fort St
Victoria, BC, Canada, V8V 3K2
www.friesenpress.com

Copyright © 2015 by Marnie Hill
First Edition — 2015

All rights reserved.

No part of this publication may be reproduced in any form, or by any means, electronic or mechanical, including photocopying, recording, or any information browsing, storage, or retrieval system, without permission in writing from the publisher.

ISBN
978-1-4602-6211-5 (Hardcover)
978-1-4602-6212-2 (Paperback)
978-1-4602-6213-9 (eBook)

1. Self-Help, Spiritual

Distributed to the trade by The Ingram Book Company

Table of Contents

A Little About Me (Introduction) vii

My Dedications. xix

The Soul & Spirit 1

Embraced By An Angel 4

Childhood And Souls In The Afterlife 8

Dealing With Loss 15

Our Soul Families 20

Whispers From The Soul 25

The Importance Of Soul Healing 41

A Soul's Wake-Up Call 47

Energy Healing For The Soul 65

Spiritual Life Coaching With The Afterlife 74

Intuition 85

Meditation 95

Self-Esteem And The Soul 99

Accepting My Soul's Calling 106

Warnings From The Afterlife 113

What Happens When We Die 120

Suicide And The Soul 124

Heaven Has Visiting Hours 130

Are Ghosts Real? 137

Angels & Spirit Guides 142

My Conversation With Heaven 148

Past Lives 151

Soul Healing 154

"My past has strengthened me; it has allowed me to celebrate the beauty that is within my soul."

A LITTLE ABOUT ME
(INTRODUCTION)

I did not wake up one day and say something obvious, like, "Hey, I want to be a medium or a psychic." In fact, when it came to the point of accepting my gifts and abilities, I fought it every step of the way. I don't believe this is a gift that is solely for specific people. I do believe it's a gift, though. We are all gifted in something. As for the gift of being a medium, a person needs to believe in the spirit world, have courage to connect with the Afterlife, and, if she/he is going to do this work professionally, have a deep desire to help people and the souls in Heaven.

Based on the experiences I have had, I feel the spirit world has chosen me to do this work; it was not me choosing to do this work. Ever since I can remember, Spirit has been making its presence known and trying to get my attention — trying to show me that my connection with the Afterlife is very, very real and needed.

It's always been my decision to do what I wanted with my gift, and when I see how much it helps people, I feel blessed and honoured to be a messenger for the Afterlife. However, when I agreed to do this work, I told God I was only going to talk to the dead as long as it helped people, as I only want positive experiences for everyone — and that includes me, too!

I have always wanted to help people, even when I was a young child. When I was a teenager, I fought the idea of being a nun or a psychologist. When I started dating, the nun idea went out the window! When I began to learn and experience life, my desire to help others increased, which led me to study social work and psychology for a while. I have spent time in business focusing on sales, marketing, and employment recruiting. I always felt I had a great understanding of the human mind and soul, even from childhood. Perhaps I am an old soul!

However, there will always be something to learn and experience in life; it's mandatory for our growth and for our existence. It's why we are here.

I have volunteered for various organizations all the way from my early twenties to mid-thirties. When I was 30, I started on the road to studying psychology, which pretty much slowed down when I had my second child; however, I am still an avid learner/student today. I am a student of the human mind, the soul, and the Afterlife, and I consider myself a lifelong learner of too many disciplines.

I believe learning is essential for personal growth. I feel if you have stopped learning, you are probably on the road to Heaven, taking the next step on your soul's path and getting ready to learn once more. There is no resting in the Afterlife.

It took me many years to come to terms with my ability to "talk to the dead." I have never been trained as a psychic or a medium. I was fortunate to be able to connect with my spirit guides at an early age; they guided me to specific books, certain classes to take, and who or who not to get or stay connected with. When I look at my past today, I only wish I had learned how to listen and accept my gift at an earlier age. Life would have been so much easier! As for the world of Spirit, everything happens in God's time, not always in my time, and everything is and was as it should have been anyway.

I don't even know how it all came about, this connecting with my guides and angels. There were days when I felt lonely but not alone. I have always felt spiritual energy surrounding me. Sometimes it feels like someone is in the room or in the house with me when no physical person is ever present. Spirit energy is very different from human energy. It was a natural progression for me to finally reach out to the energies that surrounded me and to connect with them.

After I immersed myself in the Afterlife and made it a part of my personal and professional life, I noticed that some of those lonely moments I would experience when I was younger simply diminished. I have learned over the years that loneliness is simply a soul disconnected from the essence of one's life. In fact, sometimes when I finish a reading or leave a group reading, I feel like I have left a concert. Spirit can be noisy, and that can be exhausting!

Some of my teachings that help me connect with loved ones and coach others to live a better life have been brought to me in my dreams by my guides, angels, and my deceased parents — not all, but some. I use these teachings to help others today.

I have astral-travelled throughout the night on many occasions to places that have taught me about soul healing. My spiritual guides connect with me through meditation when I request them to do so, and sometimes they just show up.

When I was 5, I had my first out-of-body experience where I actually travelled throughout the house! My spirit body went into the kitchen, and there was my family having breakfast one Saturday morning. I tried to talk to them and became frustrated and afraid when they couldn't hear me. My father said out loud, "We really should try to get Marnie up. She is sleeping really late." I kept trying to tell him I was right there. My mother said she would try again. She went into my room, came out, and said I was still sleeping. Afraid, I drifted my way back to my body, which was lying in bed.

I remember all of a sudden I was trying to open my eyes up and I couldn't. I couldn't even move my body. Eventually, I woke up and went into the kitchen and told my family of my experience. They just looked at me and smiled, so I closed my mouth like I usually did and sat down to eat breakfast.

Even though I got really good at keeping my feelings and my experiences quiet, the spirit world, particularly my female guide, would tell me not to worry. I was told I was okay, and I was not to be afraid of any of the experiences I was having while I was awake or while I was dreaming, as it would all make sense one day. I didn't realize how long it was going to take me to understand what my spirit guides exactly meant by this. They are still teaching me today! I'm convinced I will never stop learning. Teachings come in my dreams or even through my life experiences. My life lessons, dreams, and communication with the Afterlife have put me on the path of my life calling and have taught me about forgiveness, grief, and happiness.

I feel it's important to note that I am a strong believer in God, and I know that what I do is NOT against God. While I am not going to get too much into talking about religion in this book, I do believe we are all given gifts to help people, and some people are given different kinds of gifts. My focus is on service to God and the spirit world, solely to help others live a better life. I do this by utilizing my gifts and the knowledge I have gained over the years from my own experiences and the variety of training I have had within many disciplines.

Not only do I restore people's beliefs and faith in God and the Afterlife, but I can bring comfort and peace to troubled souls who have been stricken with grief and who, perhaps, can only see the dark when there is light within and all around them.

When I attend church, which is as much as I can, I get very emotional and listen with all my heart. I don't believe God is found within a church; I believe he is found within. He is within you. I mean, Jesus started his teachings on a mountain! I pray at least twice a day and thank God for my gift that helps so many. I try to live within gratitude daily!

I have a picture of Mother Mary on my wall by the stairs, and every morning I look at that and thank her. I thank her for her truth and for what she brought to this world. I do not dwell on the dark side of life; however, earlier in my life and in my career, the dark sometimes found me! Why? Because everything that lives, or has ever breathed, looks for acceptance and truly looks for ways to be a part of the light. When you delve into the other side and are a helping to guide people on this planet, you begin to shine very bright. The spirit world knows exactly how to find a medium — both the good spirits and the bad spirits.

I found over the years, when I stay close to my faith and I trust and believe in myself and the Afterlife, my life stays within the divine flow, and only good comes to me! It's a practice, and a practice well worth the work.

When I was young, I instinctively knew something was a little different about me, and not only from the "knowing" I would experience (seeing the spirit world with my physical eyes and having very vivid dreams that I know today were my guides speaking to me); I just always felt different. I have yet to find a word that would exactly describe "feeling different," where someone else may understand me and say, "Yes, I know what you mean."

I would wake up nightly to tell my parents there were people standing in my room. I remember one man very vividly saying that he really wanted to talk to me and that he had something he needed to share or teach me. I found out almost thirty years later it was my spirit guide. When I was young, I kept pulling the covers over my head, and when it got to be too much I would scream, which caused my parents to come into my room. I tried to explain to my mother and father what was happening. They insisted I was dreaming and all would be okay. I knew different, though! Of course, everything was going to be okay, but these visitations were not dreams; they were real people standing in front of me that only I could see. So I kept quiet, again.

In my teens, I learned to ignore my psychic and medium abilities only because I was afraid of what others would think of me, and I didn't want to be labeled as crazy! Around age 11, my family and I moved into a home where I saw and felt Spirit nightly. This was my grandmother's old home. I wasn't afraid of these sightings, but I didn't know what they were either, until one night that changed my life considerably. This was the night when my father acknowledged that he had seen his deceased father in the hallway on several occasions, and the dog was also sensing his energy. When he told me that, I wanted to jump for joy. For a split second, I felt a little more normal. So when I saw my father years later in the world of spirit, one evening after he had passed, I felt even more secure with my experiences. In my twenties, I acknowledged my gift, but I didn't listen to it; I kept it all a secret and lived through hell because of it. No one knew about what I could see or do except for the friends who were beginning to ask questions like, "How did you know that was going to happen?" I guess I was in the closet, so to speak.

In my thirties, I learned to live with my gift, still not understanding its purpose. In my forties, I learned to finally accept my gift, understand it, and embrace all that God, the spirit world, and the universe had to offer me. Let me tell you, though, it wasn't all about acceptance; Spirit was coming forward to me, showing up daily in my life, and my abilities were at an all-time high! There was no way I could ignore my gifts anymore. No, my calling was revealing itself once more. Spirit was speaking loud and clear, and my soul ... well, my soul was screaming at me to pay attention to my life calling.

When I finally surrendered to God and the Afterlife and agreed that I would be a messenger for the other side, it was then that I felt I was truly born. I felt I was finally born into a world where I could be me, not feel afraid of who I was, and understand that I wasn't different at all. I could educationally and consciously understand that my abilities and gifts were something I should NOT fear but EMBRACE — and that I was definitely not crazy!

I feel my gift is here to help everyone: the living, the dead, and myself. However, I am like anyone else, and I need to work through my own problems. I don't get lottery numbers or anything like that. Why on earth would any spirit or angel provide that to me, or to anyone else for that matter? It would take me, and you, away from the number one rule of life: learning!

I can hear the subtle voices of my mother and father and my guides, who usually say *yes, no, turn right, turn left,* and so on. This information is only provided to me if it's for my highest power or is helping someone. That is, if I need to learn something, I am going to learn it like everyone else! It's a great responsibility to conduct this type of work — delivering messages from the Afterlife and intuitively and psychically helping people. I am open to all sorts of energies and entities and to beautiful light, angels, and loved ones who have very important information and love to provide to me and to my clients.

God, spirit guides, angels, and your loved ones in the spirit world will protect you always. They will never do you harm. However, it's important to remember the spirit world can only help you if you help yourself and ask for GUIDANCE. I have capitalized the word *guidance* because the spirit world is not meant to interfere with your life or provide you with things or opportunities. You need to learn how to help yourself and be in alignment to receive the opportunities that may come forward to you.

It's interesting, though — the more I do this work, the more I realize that the darkest energies seem to reside within the human mind, not within the souls in the Afterlife. Dark energies lie within the body of the ego that is within everyone who is alive. This is something that scares me the most. People are far more capable of hurting someone than any spirit ever could, and Spirit never lies — the good Spirit anyway! I have realized today that anything that takes you away from love, respect for all, and universal kindness and that produces negative judgment may be the biggest evil of all. Maybe it's the devil who seeks to find surrender within all of us, the spirit who looks to cause pain, scrutiny, and lack of forgiveness.

Since we are all intuitive on some level, I do encourage people to learn how to embrace their intuitive side, as intuition is a gift that has been given to everyone from birth. Listening to it can be a hard lesson to learn; however, it is worth it!

I have often wondered if people who have been born with a high degree of psychic or mediumship ability may have something structurally different within their brains that allows them to adapt to the process of connecting with the other side more easily than others. When you look into the lives of other mediums and psychics, you begin to notice that the ability to talk to the dead seems to follow through within families — not all, but some. However, psychic ability is of the mind, and the soul is of the mind, too, so perhaps it's our souls talking to us and providing us psychic information. The stronger the soul, the stronger the calling, the stronger the heart. But does that mean it is easier to receive messages from the Afterlife? I will talk more about the differences in intuition, psychic abilities, and medium abilities later in the book.

One day while sitting in silence and contemplating if this was something I really should do — "talking to the dead," that is — I heard a voice, very loud and clear, say from the other side, "This is a gift that has been given to you. Why don't you accept it?" We may not all be destined to be mediums or psychics, like I feel I have been, but each of us has been chosen to follow a path as part of the soul's calling.

I have found over the years, however, that when you start talking about getting gifts from Heaven, it not only raises some eyebrows, it causes many people's egos to take a turn for the worse and begin the journey of jealousy and hate against those gifted with an extrasensory ability.

Some people are natural-born athletes and leaders; you can see what they are meant to do from a very early age. While others have to try and work hard to develop their skills, some people are simply born with a high degree of abilities and IQ! I am not here to tell you what to think about mediums or psychics or the Afterlife, for that matter. It's important for you to make up your own mind on what mediums, psychics, and the Afterlife mean to you.

Over the years, I have noticed that I have received some information that is parallel in all of my readings. For instance, our loved ones will tell us anything we need to hear to help us on our journey. I have to emphasize *need;* one will always receive the information one needs, not necessarily the information one feels one wants. However, your loved ones will come forward with evidential information to verify their existence with details about themselves when they were alive and will provide information about you that only you would know. If you, yourself, do not have good intentions about the reading and are coming into the reading carrying a large amount of negativity and fear, it not only makes the situation difficult for the medium, but your loved ones or angels may decide not to speak during this time; you need to have the purest of intentions for the spirit world to communicate freely with you.

Spirit can see everything. If you are scared or trying to block the information (because of fear), the information may come through slower or Spirit may disconnect from the reading altogether.

A LITTLE ABOUT ME (INTRODUCTION)

Spirit's intention is all about love, not about pain.

For myself, I only deal with the highest level of energies, meaning God, angels closest to God, and loved ones in Heaven. The spirit world doesn't want to hurt me or deliver negative messages for me to have to channel. If I enter into a reading and someone starts yelling, glaring at me, or talking negatively to me, that negativity can go directly to my chakra and cause me real physical pain — a lesson I had to learn at the beginning of my journey as a medium.

Learning about spiritual protection and knowing how the spirit world protects me has helped me tremendously. Delivering messages for the Afterlife is serious business, and once I experienced the true essence of Spirit and began to deliver healing messages that helped so many, I realized I couldn't turn away from God's work; it's next to impossible, and I wouldn't want to either! So I am in it for the long term. I can't turn myself off to the spirit world, and if I go longer than two weeks without doing readings, not only does it cause chaos within my energy body, but Spirit shows up everywhere!

If I go out to the mall, for example, I can hear the spirit world trying to talk to me. If I go and get my hair done, I can pretty much bet a loved one is going to show up and ask me to deliver a message. I can honestly say that talking to the dead grounds me — as long as I am following through with my calling and delivering messages for the Afterlife, that is!

When I do a reading, not only do I use all my senses, such as clairvoyance, clairaudience, claircogniance, clairalience, clairgustance, and clairempathy, but I am also an empath. This is something I was naturally born with; one can't learn to be an empath, and it's not just about exercising empathy, either. It means I can feel other people's pain and pain in the spirit world, but I can't remove it. Those afflicted have to learn how to work through the pain themselves so it doesn't affect their lives or health.

Earlier in my career, the energies of other people, not just the energies of Spirit, really affected me. In those initial days, I had to send a strong intention and pray to God and the spirit world to provide me only with people who needed and would benefit from my readings and healings — people who really wanted to speak with their loved ones and truly needed guidance. Guess what? They listened and delivered! Thanks again, Spirit! I became much happier doing this kind of work when I set my own boundaries and requested, "No troublemakers, please!"

During my journey of self-acceptance, I have learned how my past has strengthened me. Everything I have ever experienced has brought me to where I am today, along with my strength and courage to live life to the fullest and to do this kind of spiritual work. With each negative experience I endured in the past, I looked within and saw the lesson, shook off my fear, and said that no matter what happens, I will never stop doing God's work. Believe me, God heard me each time! I became even stronger, not weaker so that I would stop speaking to the dead, which was the intention of the negative people I had encountered earlier in my career. I should be thanking all those individuals who gave me a rough time in the beginning. I am where I am today because I have not only learned these lessons but can see how the light always wins over the dark. My experience to date has shown me that you may come in being a non-believer, but you will leave being a believer and be much happier for it!

I understand skeptics, as I, too, was once a non-believer, but science is making great strides in discovering how powerful the human mind is. We have so much potential as human beings! One day we will have a clearer understanding of the intuitive mind and its capabilities and a greater understanding of the other side, death, and life after death. Again, this is my belief system; if you also want to embrace it, I welcome you to it. We all have the power to believe whatever we choose to believe. This is called free will, or freedom of choice.

I wanted to let you know that I wrote this book for one reason and one reason only: to help you by providing you with a little inspiration and hope! I didn't have to dig up my past, revisit my old wounds that have already healed, or open my life up to the rest of the world for money, glory, or even acceptance; at this stage of my life, I really couldn't care less about what anybody thinks of me or what anybody has to say about me.

A LITTLE ABOUT ME (INTRODUCTION)

I learned very quickly in life that no matter how good you are, no matter how much you try to make things right, somebody is always going to have an opinion of you, good or bad. Some people are going to try to prove you wrong to satisfy their own egos and say, "I told you I was right," because they need that kind of approval and acceptance in this world. I feel sorry for their souls. I am who I am, and I love myself and my life! I am a medium, I am a psychic, I have been connected to spirit world since I was 5, and I can read messages from your soul.

I feel at home when I help people and talk to the other side. When I guide someone through grief and help others increase their self-esteem to awaken to the realization that they have the power to create the life they desire, it brings me great comfort.

It took me many years to understand why every time I tried to get another job, change my career, or take another course, nothing seemed to work. There was always something happening in my life that would bring me back to my true calling: speaking to Heaven and helping the soul! I realize today, and I hope you will too, that no one has to live in pain or fear; everyone needs to accept themselves and understand they are in control of their lives and can get on the road to happiness. Life is for the living; there is so much in this world to understand or experience!

We were not born to exist and then die. No, we are all here for so much more. Each one of our souls has a purpose, and everything you have experienced is here to teach you something about love. When your body dies, your soul lives on. You never stop living or stop growing. I hope this book will help you awaken to your higher power so you can start creating happiness in your life. I know this sounds easier than it is, but if I can do it, so can you!

I have lost many close people in my life. I have endured divorce, poverty, emotional and physical abuse, and illness. I made it through everything. I was meant to make it through everything so I could learn about me and my life and teach others from my experiences. God and the spirit world helped me every step of the way. One of the most powerful elements of life is knowing the self and then, in return, knowing others so you can help them.

I believe we are all right in the middle of Heaven and each one of us is a co-creator of his or her own life. For years, many people bang their heads against the walls of their world, trying to figure out why they are here, who they are, the meaning of life, and the meaning of *their* lives. Well, I can honestly say we won't know the truth about many things until we pass over into the light; it is then we will learn the real truth about religion, life, and ourselves. However, in this life, you do have a calling, a purpose, and if you listen to the *whispers from the soul,* they will tell you what you need, where you need to go, and how you need to heal.

Coming to terms with this, though, isn't as simple as it seems. Many individuals may need to go through a healing process first to be able to embrace their reasons for incarnating at this specific time. I will discuss this later throughout these pages.

Today and every day when I wake up, I realize my life is beginning. Every morning, life brings me an opportunity and the power to write my own story, to pave the way for my life and my future. Life is a never-ending story, full of twists and turns, happiness and sadness; it all depends on how you respond to the situation at hand that creates the outcome for your next chapter.

There are no mistakes in life, and each one of us is exactly where he or she is supposed to be! We are all special, and each one of us has a unique calling to fulfill with his or her soul and with God. If this book has found you, then you are ready to realize that you are not alone in this world and that the experiences you have endured have a reason and a purpose. You are now ready to embark on a journey of self-realization, which I hope will take you into a dimension of fulfillment. Keep love in your heart, as we are here to live life to its fullest without pain, judgment, fear, or hate of the self and of others. **There are no accidents in this life; instead, there are lessons!**

I hope you enjoy my book. I wrote this from my heart, not from a scholarly view. The words within this book are about my own healing and experiences. I hope it brings you healing and an understanding of yourself, of your soul, and perhaps even of the Afterlife. Blessings to you,

......Marnie

MY DEDICATIONS

I dedicate this book to my soul family: my husband Dwayne and my two beautiful sons. Dwayne, you are my rock. I love you so much. Thank you for being my best friend. To my two beautiful boys, you are truly old souls and on this journey with me. Every time I look at you or hear your voices, I am reminded of the power of God! To my parents, both of your lives were so shortly lived. I know you are with me and with my family every step of the way, helping us and guiding us on this incredible journey we call life, all from the other side.

To my spirit guides and angels, thank you for being a part of my soul contract. I know at times I didn't listen as well as I should, but I am getting there, and I thank you for guiding me in getting this booked published. Finally, thank you, God! In the depths of my despair, I always felt your loving energy surround me. You never once left me, and you always gave me strength, even when I felt I had no more left within me. Isabelle, my guardian angel, I heard your voice that night and felt your wings of protection wrap around me when I thought I was on my last and final road. Joe, my spirit guide, thank you for showing me the way. I listened!

I also dedicate this book to you, the reader. To everyone who has ever lost someone or something and believed that life felt too unbearable to live. To the individuals who have experienced abuse from someone they loved and trusted, and for the ones who are downright scared to be themselves — perhaps it is in one of these pages you will find or experience the realization that there is more to you and to this life, to understand that our loved ones only change form when they die. And most importantly to you, may you remember you are loved and beautiful the way God created you. You are never alone!

Please note, all names and places have been changed to protect the privacy of others. The information provided in this book is designed to provide helpful information on the subjects discussed. This book is not meant to be used, nor should it be used, to diagnose or treat any medical condition. For diagnosis or treatment of any medical problem, consult a physician. The information I have received for this book has come from my own soul and the world of spirit.

a soul's journey
───

THE SOUL & SPIRIT

I feel it's important to provide you with some information about the soul and spirit.

The soul is the essence of who we are and who we have been in our past lives. It carries the knowledge of many lifetimes, the many lessons we have learned, and the many lessons we are to learn. The soul is like a blueprint for the spirit. The spirit is what carries "energy" to the soul; one cannot exist without the other. You may have heard the terms *higher consciousness, higher power,* and *higher self;* these are essences of the soul.

The soul is of the mind, and the mind carries all capabilities. The mind, body, and spirit are all interconnected. Each is a level and needs the others to stay alive. Each needs to be strong to remain in human form. Living within balance of all three allows us to be completely connected to life and to our souls — the ultimate level. When we are connected to the soul, we become connected to the divine that is within all of us. Then we can experience, with a clear mind and an open heart, the divinity that is also around us. In reality, we are connected or "plugged in" to life. However, not everyone can reach the fourth level, the soul level.

Your source of energy becomes stronger when you become connected to your soul. It is then that you have the ability to connect to the higher self and possibly to the outer universal energies.

Does it sound easy to do? Well, it isn't, and it can take many lifetimes to get it right. However, you can also get it right in one lifetime; it all depends on how hard you work at it!

Some people are naturally more connected to universal energies and to their souls. They may have spent many lifetimes on the treadmill of life — learning, experiencing, and growing.

Each one of us has a *soul contract;* this is a contract you made with yourself and God before you were born. Sometimes this is also referred to as your *Akashic Record.* Within these records lay your life purpose and your lessons within this life. It is up to you to learn how to overcome these lessons, heal the soul, and remove all karmic energy attachments within this lifetime. If you succeed at overcoming all the lessons needed within this lifetime, your soul may go on to live other lives; and if your soul has reached its last time around, your soul may be ready to embark on a new level and journey by becoming a spirit guide in the Afterlife.

Can you imagine what it would be like to become a guide on the other side, helping people from the spirit world based on the knowledge you have gained over your lifetime? It's pretty remarkable stuff when you think about it!

Your soul contract determines what experiences you will have in this lifetime. It was determined before you were born; this means that birth, marriage, illness, life partners, situations you find yourself in, and death are all part of your soul contract. However, in your soul contract are clauses — yes, I said *clauses.* If you are a quick learner and are learning through your life situations, you can maneuver through your life quickly. This doesn't mean you will die more quickly, however; it simply means you will be able to experience and explore more of what is in your soul contract.

The downside is that if you don't learn the lessons you set out to learn, you will keep trying to learn them in this lifetime and into your next life. That's why many of us find ourselves in the same predicament over and over again. We didn't learn from the last situation, so the lesson has manifested again, just in a different form. Let's say you meet Mr. or Ms. Wonderful, and you fall in love quickly. Perhaps you entered into the relationship quicker than you should have, since you just lost your last relationship or were experiencing some form of loss. Mr. Wonderful or Ms. Wonderful may start out great in the beginning, simply to turn out just like your last relationship, leaving you bitter and a little confused.

Ever hear someone say they keep meeting the same type of person over and over again? It's like they are blind to love. Well, in essence, the person partially is and is probably blind to the life lessons that were put within their soul contract. The same goes for their career or health — and the list can go on.

So you may be asking what, then, is Spirit. *Spirit* is an energy force that sits within the soul and is the fuel for the body. When your body dies, Spirit and soul become one. Most people refer to that as the spirit world; however, I like to refer these entities as *souls in the Afterlife*.

The bodies we have chosen to live within are vessels for the soul. This is why when your spirit is low and your physical body isn't feeling well, you feel energetically drained. When there are no other physical reasons for your experiences, you need look within the soul and seek the answers that lie within. This will allow you to heal and grow from your experiences and to receive wholeness. You can see how important it is to take care of the physical body; it's your ultimate link!

In the following pages, you will learn how valuable your current life is and your previous life experiences have been. You will begin to understand that life gives you lessons continually. If you haven't learned a lesson, the lesson to be learned will continually make itself known, manifesting in different areas of your life.

Bad things happen to good people, good things happen to bad people, and good things happen to good people. It's all part of the cycle of life. Everything is always as it should be. The greatest lesson is learning how to accept it, embrace it, understand it, and then change it so it can not only help you but also help another person. It's a powerful thing when you take your life lessons and turn them around to help another soul. In fact, I have been told time and time again from souls in the Afterlife that this is exactly how it should be; this is the true essence of living.

EMBRACED BY AN ANGEL

I was in my late twenties, and as I lay on the floor gasping for my very last breath — or so it seemed — I looked up around me to see the home that my second husband and I had built. I saw the colours of the décor and smelled the new carpet right under my nose. I looked up at this man who had said he loved me five years earlier, and I had believed him. Yet today he was laughing while kicking me in the chest and saying, "I hope you die, %^&*!"

I couldn't breathe. I tried to get up and I couldn't. I felt like I was going to die. I couldn't understand this man whom I had married, how he didn't know or realize he was killing me. I became so afraid. I thought this was it, and I remember thinking, *No way am I going to die like this.* All of a sudden, I heard the words of a woman: "It's okay. It's almost over, child. You will never have to experience this again. It is done." As the words were filling my head full of hope, I felt a huge, comfortable, loving energy surround me. It felt like wings wrapping around me, cocooning me with protection. Not knowing what I was experiencing, I began to feel a large amount of energy building up inside me. With so much energy, I got up and started to run out of the house. As I ran out of the house, I said, "This is the last time you will ever touch me!" And it was.

Terrified and desperately wanting to get away from that whole situation, I headed out the door, jumped in my vehicle, and began to drive, knowing this was going to have to end. I knew I needed to get out of this marriage; he would never change. We would continue to be destructive together if I stayed. I may not have another opportunity to run. I may end up dead.

What was I to do, though? I was scared, I had no money because he had cleaned out the bank account on numerous occasions, and to top it off, I had recently been laid off of work. Where was I to go?

Not only did I feel like a failure, but I was also very mad at myself, as I was in the same predicament again! Love had somehow blinded me again, and I had lost good judgment.

After I left the house, I drove around for at least a couple of hours, hoping when I got back to the house he would be gone. He was. Thank God!

I went into the house. I felt like I was on the verge of a breakdown. I took as much as I could of my clothes and headed off towards another province.

I felt completely terrified, ashamed, and exhilarated at the same time; there was a small piece of me that finally felt free, perhaps even safe, once more. As I drove, the music was blaring. I wanted to drown out my own thoughts. I had to come to terms with what was happening in my life. I needed to wake up and to start living healthier. I was tired of arguing, tired of being afraid, and tired of not knowing where my life was going. I knew I was worth so much more and capable of doing so much more with my life.

After doing all of this deep thinking while I was driving, it felt like a wheel was constantly turning inside of my head. Feelings of fear and regret were trying to overcome me. Then, all of a sudden, I got this huge jolt. It felt like someone had given me a slap on the face. At that moment, I was brought back to what I had experienced earlier — to the energy that had surrounded me when I thought I was going to die. I wondered, *Who was talking to me?* Where had this voice I heard come from? As I drove, everything started coming back to me. The voice I had heard earlier kept playing back to me in my head. I pulled over and realized I had no bruises on my body where I had been kicked. I hurt, and there was some redness, but no bruises or broken ribs were visible where there should have been some. I had been close to being unconscious; I recalled that I couldn't even breathe.

Then, as I was doing a life review on myself, I realized this wasn't the first time I had heard a voice when I was experiencing pain or was about to. I remembered when I had been driving down the highway one day in my early twenties and was behind a large truck. I saw a stack of insulation in the back of the truck that was completely open. I heard, "Move to the right lane," and I did. Within a second, those bundles of insulation began to fall out of the back of the truck. I was going 100 kilometers an hour, and I would have been seriously hurt if I hadn't moved my car into the other lane.

During that drive after leaving my second husband, I was putting so much together. I remembered all the other times I saw spirits, had that knowing sense, or when I heard voices from "the other side." I couldn't understand why I was in such disbelief! I had encountered Spirit in different ways so many times before. I had heard my name, and I had heard other things from the other side, but I had never felt what I had felt that day. A warm energy protected me from harm. It was an experience that seemed to take every other fear, physical pain, and painful thought away at that specific time.

Due to the denial of my gift, it would be many years until I would truly understand what it was I had experienced. Hearing the voice and feeling angel wings wrap around me would one day drastically change my life forever. Was my soul, my spirit — me — finally ready to embrace the true essence of my being, my authentic self, and my soul's destiny? It would take some time, trust, spiritual healing, forgiveness, and believing in a higher power before I could set my life straight, and that is exactly what I began to do.

The path I endured would take me almost ten years of personal healing and growth. Yes, ten years! Why so long? It would take years of understanding to realize that I had many lives that I had lived before and that this life was to be my last time around on this earth. I also had to raise my self-esteem. All of my karma, all of my remaining life lessons, were to be lived within this lifetime. As of today, I know of several past lives that I have lived, and I understand from my higher self and my guides that I am an old soul — a soul that has been living for hundreds of years, maybe thousands.

Now, if you had told this to me when I was 27 or even in my early thirties, I would have thought you were crazy and probably would have kept away from you for a while. But since my soul knows best, I would have eventually come around, and I did.

In this book lie my personal struggles and my victories. I have written about all my experiences, which have allowed me to develop my spiritual life coaching program called the Soul Enhancement™ Life Coaching Program. This program has been designed for you to start living a better life by bringing wellness to your soul. It's not going to take you ten years, like it took me. What I teach has been tried and tested by yours truly, and as of today, it has worked for many individuals.

Please note that the coaching program is not within the book, though I have offered some specific tools to help you on your journey of healing. I understand the true meaning of "When the student is ready, the teacher will arrive." You become a student when you are conceived, and every person, situation, and experience is your teacher, teaching you the ways of the heart, as the heart is the doorway to the soul.

So was it my angel I heard earlier, who wrapped its wings around me to protect me? I know it was. We all have angels and spirit guides, guiding us on this path. Your life has been predetermined before your soul entered into the human body. Everything happens for a reason, as every situation or person you meet within this lifetime is meant to be. I know this can be hard to swallow, but the gift is the fact that you have a choice with your experiences. You have a choice to either become a victim or learn how to maneuver through the situation to keep your soul aligned with all of life — this is alignment within love. I will explain later in the book about how death and illness are all part of the soul's plan and how you can either change the outcome or delay it in order for the soul to continue to grow. It takes understanding to realize that sometimes this is the plan. I understood it on the night my life changed forever.

CHILDHOOD AND SOULS IN THE AFTERLIFE

I grew up in a small town. My childhood, most would say, was a little rocky. My mother, through most of my youth, was in and out of the hospital, bless her soul. She suffered from severe depression and other disorders, and she committed suicide right after I turned 7. Yet she was very gifted. I know this by thinking back to some of the things she would tell me when I was a child.

Today I have often thought perhaps she, too, could see "dead people" or the "other side," and in the '70s, this was not a common way of being or thinking. I remember her talking to me and letting me know she felt and saw so much all the time, and it hurt her. Many times, I had to ask myself, *What if she had all of this stuff going on, stuff she was highly sensitive to, and had no idea how to deal with it?* I have asked this question many times! There were no tools for her or those with her gifts, not like there are today. My own guides have given me the answer that she was in fact a sensitive and a medium but one who also had a very difficult childhood. She was a person who was taught fear was okay and to live within emotional and spiritual pain, which resulted in her mental illness.

What matters most to me is that she is at peace; she is one of my guardians. She made her presence known to me one evening. From her, I know that it's up to me to live my life the best way and healthiest way I can. It's my "soul" responsibility, no one else's. Her death did not impact me as badly as I thought. I was sad, but somehow I knew she was in a place that could help her — a place where she could laugh, not cry. After she passed away, I always felt her loving presence. I knew everything was going to be okay in my life and that one day I would see her again, which I did. I miss her, though, and there isn't a day that goes by that I don't think of her or my father. I can keep them alive within my memories and within my heart — that is something no one can ever take away from me.

Through her death, I have been able to understand and receive information regarding suicide and the Afterlife, which I will also share later in this book. My mother's passing brought me opportunities, growth, and comfort with the Afterlife. After all, I feel blessed to know that she is now one of my own spiritual guides helping me and guiding me through life.

When I was a child, I spent most of my days playing with toys in my room. Cut-outs were the thing back then — paper dolls with paper clothes. It was fun; I really had to engage in my own creativity. I also learned how to cook, do the laundry, and take care of myself, since my father worked full time. My mother was not well most days. I needed to learn how to take care of things. I remember my mother spent most of her days sleeping or crying, but I loved her every minute, and nothing could ever change that. In fact, when I look back today, I actually enjoyed being alone, which is not much different from how I am today. I love peace and quietness, but at the time I had to grow up fast. It would be years later that I would understand that much of my inner healing would need to be focused on these specific times: my early years.

During my healing, it was important for me to remember that I was an old soul who had lived many lifetimes and that this also contributed to my inner knowing of things. I seemed to have knowledge that I was never taught before in my current life, specifically regarding the mind and the soul.

After my mother passed away, I lived with my grandparents for a while and I started at a new school. My father would come home on weekends until he was able to transfer to our new location. I was still adjusting well to everything even though I was shy and very sensitive to my surroundings (meaning I felt things other children didn't). I seemed to pick up quickly on other people's moods or whether their intentions were good or bad. When something happened that would show me what I felt was right, this kept me feeling safe — safe within my own knowledge and understanding of the world around me.

It was hard being in grade two. The children kept asking where my mother was. I would make up a story, which would follow me through into my late twenties, that my mother was killed in a car crash. It was so much less confusing for everyone, and I was sure that if I told the truth, I would be judged — and it turned out I was judged later on in my life but only by people who lived within a world of fear and misunderstanding regarding mental illness.

I didn't have a lot of close friends, yet I had many friends. I think because I was so shy, I was scared to speak up in class. Today, I would be considered a sensitive child or an indigo child — an old soul. Personally, I think I am both a humanist and an interdimensional indigo. I believe this type of child has been around for hundreds of years. It's just that today we are more consciously aware and open to viewing personality traits and abilities in a different light, and there is so much more information available today than when I was growing up.

It was confusing for me back then. It was the '70s, and no books or literature was available for what I was experiencing and would experience through my life. So I kept my feelings and experiences to myself because I was certainly not going to express them at that time, not with what happened to my mother. Additionally, I was very scared of causing any type of chaos in my father's life. I knew he was sad about losing his wife — my mother. I also knew that my parents had not been getting along and had at one point discussed divorce, which caused a lot of fear within my life.

One evening my parents sat me down at the dinner table and said that they were going to get a divorce and that I needed to pick which parent I would reside with. What a heart-wrenching time! My mother said she would commit suicide if she didn't have me live with her. At that moment, I was wondering why the help she was getting wasn't working. It was obvious to me, at age 6, that the medications she was taking were clearly not benefitting her, but my hands felt tied. Reluctant and fearful, I did not want to choose, so I asked if I could live with them both and ran to my room.

My room always felt like a safe haven for me. Sometimes I would sit at my bed playing with my dolls, and I would feel this beautiful, safe energy surround me.

Even though I felt surrounded by light, I am still human and have the same emotions as everyone. I was still a child — a child who seemed to see a lot of mistrust in the physical world. I know today that if I had been able to speak freely about my experiences with Spirit when I was young and to express what was happening to me, my self-esteem would have been a lot higher than it was. It's very difficult for children to have spiritual experiences and not be able to freely express their opinions or talk about them. Many times children feel other people don't or won't understand them; this belief can come from many different sources, and it's not productive.

I feel it's important at this point to speak briefly about Spirit (souls in the Afterlife) and children. Children are very intuitive and can connect effortlessly with Spirit; however, this ability can change quickly when children grow and their surroundings do not allow them to embrace the possibility. You can say encouraging things to them. *Yes, it was Grandma or Grandpa you saw last night! And it's okay that they came from Heaven to visit you! Isn't it wonderful God gives our loved ones opportunities once in a while to stop in and say hello?*

I think we are getting better as a society and are learning how to embrace the possibilities that there really is more to this life and that maybe Heaven is real! When it comes to children and the spirit world, things can get a little sticky and quite tricky. Parents must remember that children must follow their own paths in this lifetime and that parents are simply there to protect them and allow them to experience many paths for their own personal growth.

I have met some parents who want to develop their children's medium abilities, in hopes they will continue to talk to the dead later on. This is a very, very dangerous path to lead a child down. I know firsthand that the mind can only handle what it is meant to handle! You can't force someone to see or keep from seeing Spirit, if it's not the soul's intention and if the child doesn't want to — not to mention the fact that children are also very creative; if they think they are getting some sort of benefit from either scaring the parent or if the parent is making them feel special because of seeing things in the Afterlife, they may continue to dream up visitations and sightings when they are not really happening. It takes knowledge to understand the world of Spirit, and children don't have the knowledge to carry out continual conversations with the dead and not let it affect them on a conscious and spiritual level.

I think it's wonderful and such a gift when children connect with the other side. It's important to let them know that their angels, guides, and loved ones who are in Heaven are simply stopping in and letting them know they are okay and that they are protecting the children from the other side. Visitations from the Afterlife can be a bit scary for an adult, let alone a small child. So let your children know they have a safe place in which to talk to you, and don't press them too much on what was said. Let them tell you their experiences, allowing them to feel safe and secure with everything.

If it does get to out of hand and Spirit is around too much, simply do a prayer and ask that the spirit world not come around at this time. Thank the spirits and let them know you love them! The world of Spirit will oblige, and they will come back when or if your child is ready. You can also place an angel or a cross beside your child's bed to keep protection over him or her. Remember, don't press the situation or keep asking; let the child come to you with the conversation.

Being a medium really is a calling, and many times it's the soul's decision to be a messenger for the Afterlife, which has been set forth long before that soul reincarnated in this lifetime. Mediumship is more than just simply seeing your loved ones; it is about the communication that happens during the event. Can the information be relayed to others? The communication must stay within a continual stream of validation and provide important healing and informative instruction to the living. It's important to remember that if your child is seeing the other side, the communication will be positive and help the child or the deceased. If your child is scared and something is emotionally hurting him or her, then you need to take some sort of action to put your child at ease, as all spirit communication should be about love.

However, there are dark energies out there in our physical and spiritual world. If parents are involved in excessive drinking, abuse, hanging out at bars, or using drugs, they can bring home some negative energy that can drain their life force. Energy is around everyone; it is also called the *aura*. Negative energy can stay within the home and within the family until it is cleared. It's important to note that negative energy or spirits can't attach themselves to healthy and happy people, and they *can't* manipulate the mind to make you do something you shouldn't do. They can make you feel miserable, though! It's another reason to live your life with peace and happiness!

If your child continues throughout his or her life saying he or she sees things and hear things and these spirits are telling your child to do bad things, it is suggested that you immediately seek psychological attention for your child. This *may* be an indication of a mental disorder such as schizophrenia. I will always refer to the fact that communication with Spirit is to be approached delicately; it's not about fun and games when you are dealing with the other side.

I know some of you may be thinking that perhaps I had negative energy attached to me from the very beginning because of my mother's mental illness and the difficulties within my parents' marriage. After all, on one rare occasion, I did have a person who claimed to be a follower of God suggest that perhaps I was a demon in disguise! If you are a child of God, which we all are (though some lose sight of that), you would never, ever accuse anyone of being a demon in this day and age. Your thought process should be about love; isn't that what Jesus has instructed us within his teachings? I don't think the devil has enough power or ability to sit within a human body for long. After all, your body is God's creation, which is full of love.

Demons don't pray to God, use rosaries, wear the cross, go to church, or want to help people! So please be careful with what you say to your children about them seeing loved ones from the Afterlife. You may permanently damage their self-esteem and emotional and physical well-being — not to mention their souls — by bringing negativity into spirit communication! There is absolutely nothing evil about delivering messages from the Afterlife and guiding a person through his or her life, as long as the information is positive, provides hope and truth, and does not cause fear. I have always told people, when I speak to the other side, that it is then that I feel closest to God, so negativity can't exist within my readings.

DEALING WITH LOSS

After my mother passed, our babysitter became very close to our father. We really enjoyed her company, and she was so much fun to be around. I know this may sound strange, the babysitter becoming close with my father, but it did happen! We all need and want love in our lives. She was a good person, and I know they both loved each other, as their love grew over time. They just were not meant to stay in love with each other, not forever.

I think my father fell in love way too soon after my mother passed. As people, we have a tendency in this life to replace loss with something or someone quickly, in the hope of helping us recover from grief. A person in pain can easily gravitate to another person, place, or thing that will fill the empty hole inside his or her soul. A person going through grief may truly believe finding love again will heal the wound that lies within his or her heart. Sadly, it can't. A soul must heal first, before it can move forward; another person or situation can't take the emotional pain away from grief. When the soul and heart are filled with self-love and healing, it is then that you can move forward from loss.

We are always bringing forward people and situations that match or resonate with our energy fields and vibrations, as we are always learning. When a soul has been healed, it begins to resonate at a healthy vibration. This vibration is also within your aura, allowing the soul to gravitate and bring forward others and life events that match the vibration of the soul.

But I know my dad also had many fears of being alone. He had two small children to take care of, and I don't even remember daycares being around when I was young! My father and the babysitter were engaged for a year before they called it off. It was a very difficult time in my life, as I had to go through the pain of losing her also — the pain of losing a mother figure all over again. I had called her *Mom*. I didn't see her again until my father passed when I was 17. She became a godsend to me later on in life. She helped me move forward with my personal life, and she became a solid structure and friend for many years — and, happily, she still is today! Something good can come from something we may see as negative; it just depends on how you view it and what role you decided to play within it: *victim* or *survivor*.

My father would eventually marry another lady, who in my opinion gave new meaning to the word *stepmother*. I could never understand her or her life, and maybe I wasn't supposed to, but I harbour no ill feelings towards her. Today, I send love to the memory and situation whenever it is brought up or thought about, though I haven't seen or heard from her in almost thirty years.

All that I experienced within both of these relationships would allow me to see the strength within myself and help me endure much diversity at such an early age. I was happy that these experiences didn't make my soul hard or angry — not even a little bit. These relationships and experiences taught me about love, acceptance, and forgiveness at a very early age. Today, this is something I can be proud of — proud that no circumstance can ever change me for the worse; it can change me only for the better.

Today within my teachings, I coach and guide others to ensure that they harbour no ill feelings from their past. The worst thing you can do in life is have negative thoughts about another person or a situation and expect that these thoughts will NOT create illness within your life. You do have to visit the past in order to realize where it is you need to go.

As I look back on my life, I realize today the different ways my family was dealing with death, and not one of those ways seem healthy. Even though we celebrated my grandfather's passing every year, the passing of my mother would never be spoken about. My stepmother would not allow any pictures of her in the house. When I was 13, I found them in a chest in the garage and asked if I could take them and put them in my room. The answer from my stepmother was a firm NO. Not understanding what this all meant, I became confused, and my mother's passing felt like a big, dirty secret we were never to talk about.

I remember when I was 15, I wanted to talk about my mother again, and my father said I was too young to understand everything. My grandmother would say that some things are best left unsaid. This brought so much discomfort into my life. I wanted to know. I needed to know. I deserved to know everything about my mother and her passing. It was like I was being taught to bury the thought and throw away the key. It was a scary time, having all of these questions going on inside my head yet not getting any help in trying to understand this yearning inside me.

It's so important to talk about the passing of your friends and family members and even the pets that pass on. Pets do go to Heaven, and sometimes a pet is the first real friend a child has. A pet is like any other family member, so you can imagine how important the grief process is when a pet passes over.

It's funny — pets keep their personalities and provide as much validation as they can from the other side. Sometimes they show me how they look and how they passed on. Animal energy is very different from human energy in the Afterlife. Their communication may be quick, and they may need to come into the reading standing beside another loved one who will help them speak.

All lives have meaning, and for one to come to the acceptance of a passing, a person must acknowledge and understand the passing and be provided with real answers — answers that have real meaning in order for a person to move forward in life. This helps tremendously with grieving, and this is why a medium can be so important in the process of grief.

At present, I honour the passing of my father and my mother every year. I have been known to set a place for Spirit to sit, and I welcome them into our home. I acknowledge their presence whenever I have a chance. Our loved ones are right beside us when we need them, so why wouldn't someone accept the essence of their souls?

When I do readings for people, not only do they get a great deal of comfort and understanding that their loved ones are in Heaven, but they are provided with validation that the souls of their loved ones are, in fact, with them. How else could I know all of this? The information coming through can be so clear that there is no doubt in anyone's mind who it is we are talking with in a session. It's wonderful when souls in the Afterlife give me their names, places where they grew up, how they look, and how they passed and keep their personalities. I love it when I get a chance to laugh with my clients and their loved ones in a reading. Mediums are here to bring peace with a passing and to help people process their grief. So honour the souls in the Afterlife and know they are always with you, helping you and guiding you; it's God's gift to you!

One of the most difficult aspects of mediumship is when I open the door to the other side and a parent comes through in hopes of having a healing with his or her child in the physical world, and the adult child doesn't want to speak with the parent. So I let the client, or *sitter* (another name for a person receiving a message), know that the parent has come forward from the spirit world and is letting us know his or her level of love for them and their family. The parent also tells us that he or she is sorry about the past and has done some healing in Heaven and simply wants the child and family members to move forward within life without negative thoughts about the family member. I have a duty as a medium, and that is not to deny Spirit's existence or messages, so if someone is in the room, you can bet Spirit is going to try and come through to say, "Hello! I love you, and I am fine!" And I am happy to deliver the information.

Many of us go through life with regrets; people regret what they have done in the past and worry if their parents or loved ones in the Afterlife can forgive them. Well, all souls that enter into Heaven learn how to forgive. My guides have told me after we acknowledge our death and have taken some time to come to terms with it (which includes seeing our death, our funeral, and our loved ones in mourning), we get an opportunity to move forward with our healing. Our souls will sit down with our guides and angels and God to determine what it is we need to heal and if we learned our lesson to move through our soul contract. It is at this time that your loved ones get an opportunity to see why you did certain things and acted certain ways in life. Everyone gets an opportunity in the Afterlife to see through the eyes of his or her loved ones. This way we can learn how to forgive and heal.

If you are carrying around heartache and pain regarding the past relationships with your loved ones, you need to get those feelings healed! Quickly! There is no time to start healing like the present, and grief is for the living; it's not for the dead. When our loved ones see that we are healing, it not only brings them peace; it also allows their healing to proceed much easier within Heaven, as they can then concentrate on bringing about their own healing.

When we die, we don't lose our feelings and emotions. We learn how to embrace them with an enlightened view of ourselves and our lives. So please don't ever think your loved ones won't understand your life, because they will and do.

OUR SOUL FAMILIES

This information I have been provided with is really eye-opening! I have been told numerous times from my own guides and the Afterlife that we actually choose our family members way before we are born; it's part of our contract with God. We choose our families, friends, and the situations we experience in this lifetime in order for our souls to learn, grow, and heal. This can sound a little crazy, but I have seen family members who have had previous lives together in the past. Depending on the situation from their previous lives, they may continue on their new path and carry with them old memories and emotions that have never cleared. The life they have today is supposed to allow them to clear it. Sadly, this isn't always the case. We live in a world that is so focused on the "me" aspect that the majority of individuals disconnect from their families as soon as they can.

I understand that there are situations that warrant a person not to be with a parent or a family member, and emotional and physical abuse is one of the first items on my list. However, too many children grow into adults carrying the energy of abuse around and never learn how to heal from it. They carry this energy and remain a victim or, even worse, become a perpetrator of abuse. It's very dangerous to remain a victim in life. By remaining a victim, the mind keeps remembering and surrendering to familiar negative situations. The mind may even be drawn to people and circumstances that allow a person to remain a victim. This can be torture. These situations can allow a person to remain in a state of what I like to refer to as *home*. For example, when a child grows up in an abusive home or a home that is filled with chaos and despair, the unhealed child grows up into an adult who is in search of the right situation to make him or her feel at "home" — where the child is a victim once again. The mind is not operating on a conscious level. The person is not purposely trying to live a life of pain; he or she just has not healed from the previous or past life experiences and actually feels more comfortable in familiar circumstances that may bring pain, allowing him or her to remain a victim. This will provide the victim with feelings of familiarity.

Subsequently, this thought proves that you can leave a person in an unhealthy position, allowing the cycle of abuse or pain to repeat until the adult child (or inner child) learns to heal from the situation. The unhealed pain may come from feeling unheard or having unresolved grief, unmet needs, abandonment issues, or unhealed past life issues — and the list goes on. Please don't go around and blame a past life or the life you had with your parents for your life today, as that isn't going to work when you are on the healing road of life. We must find a place within ourselves to forgive the situation, learn from it, and move on. You don't have to forget the situation; you do need to forgive the circumstances or the person and learn how to move forward with your life by not letting the situation interfere with your current or future life.

This process will allow you to move forward with no ill feelings or consistent negative memories regarding the person or the event. How you look at this situation and the truth of what happened is what is important, so let go of the anger. I love this quote: "The world as we have created it is a process of our thinking. It cannot be changed without changing our thinking." —Albert Einstein

So how do we go about changing our thoughts and healing?

One of the steps is to first acknowledge the situation for what it is; acknowledge that it has happened. Second, look for gratitude within the situation. You can find something to be grateful for with everything. Perhaps it's as small as allowing you to see where it is you are not meant to be. Keep that focus and look for as much gratitude as you can. Don't stop short. You being born or another person being born are things to be thankful for. So are being alive, being able to read this book, breathing … these are all factors to be grateful for. Maybe you have reached your lowest point in life and feel you have nothing left within you; be grateful for the realization of your pain, as your pain is allowing your soul to speak to you and show you where changes need to be made.

Third, look for the lesson. What has this situation brought forward to you and your life? The answer will be different for everyone. Again, what is the lesson teaching about you? When I looked at my first marriage, I realized a lot about myself and life but not enough to bring that lesson into my second marriage. It took me years of internal and spiritual healing to realize who I was and why I was here and to learn how to let go of the past and embrace the now. I learned I could co-create my life and my future from the true essence of my soul. There are many more steps you can go through within the healing process; it all depends on how you look at the situation.

For instance, I can look at the experience I had with my babysitter or my past relationships. They were painful, yet each one had many wonderful qualities within them. I have the choice to be angry about the circumstances or choose to understand the situation and then embrace the love and lesson it could offer me. If you don't learn from the situation, I can guarantee that you will keep being confronted with the same lesson.

The last step is to surrender and pray. Surrender to the circumstance and understand its reason; it will help you with the journey of forgiveness. Lastly, call in God and say a prayer for the person, for the situation, and for you. Prayer can be a powerful element to incorporate into your daily life. Simply detach from the circumstance in a healthy way. Don't forget that everyone is your teacher. Can you teach or help another person with a situation you have gone through? I bet you can — and how rewarding and powerful is that?

When I am working with clients in my coaching program, family troubles come up time and time again! In fact, we can go all the way back to childhood and heal certain feelings and emotions that we carry around within our souls today. This is why many individuals have difficulties with boundaries and have a continual need for approval from outside sources.

Have you ever heard of "inner child work"? There is validity to this type of work. I can quickly determine the specific blocks my client may have, such as past pain and experiences, as everything sits within his or her energy field. To a trained mind, the energy field can talk continuously. These blocks are not only carried within the mind; they are also carried within the heart chakra (which is the doorway to the soul). This chakra is over the heart, within the solar plexus, which is located above the upper stomach. The root chakra, which is located below the lower belly button, is also affected, leaving the entire energy body and remaining chakras out of balance. Your experiences and thoughts directly affect your chakras at all times. So as a reader of energy and the soul, I can easily pick up the blocks and help the inner child heal from past experiences. This can take a number of weeks, depending on how many situations the person has encountered. It's not only about the tools that are incorporated into the healing; it's using the right tools at the right time that allows the healing to last a lifetime. It's a bit like baking bread. If you don't put the yeast in at the right time, the whole loaf of bread will do a flop!

No, I am not saying that healing is like baking bread; that would be too easy, especially for those who have a knack for baking. What I am saying is that healing takes time and that every experience you have ever gone through with your family has meaning and a purpose. If you choose to "sweep it under the carpet" like so many families do to ignore the situation or to just let it go, it will bring you nothing but pain and probably leave you reliving a bad situation over again in another lifetime. I don't know about you, but I would rather be sitting with God and the angels than have to go through pain again with a family member I didn't trust or like. Just to let you know, this healing is your work and your work only; you don't have to even sit down with the person you are having difficulties with. Your healing is determined by the reality of the situation and your vision of the situation, and that's different for everyone. No one ever sees the event the same way.

When you see why certain circumstances have happened and apply a lesson and a healing to it, you begin to view the situation with a new set of healthy eyes. This new vision will bring you freedom, peace, and connection to your life once again! So remember, the next time you decide to let it go, sweep it under the carpet, and let those feelings and emotions burn inside you, you are creating another life lesson for yourself that will need to be relearned again, not only in another lifetime but in this lifetime too! Not to mention you could be making yourself physically sick from denying the healing process. Every circumstance you experience gives you an opportunity for healing and growth.

This is a lesson that took me many years to understand and learn how to incorporate into my life. My guides would take me to class almost every night on some occasions to teach me the most fundamental and easy way to heal what no longer serves me while allowing me to live my life with wholeness.

WHISPERS FROM THE SOUL

As I have mentioned earlier, I never told anyone about the soft whispers I would hear when I was 5. It did come to a point when I was in grade four that I asked the voices (my angels) to go away. I didn't want to hear my name anymore. I didn't want them to tell me how much they loved me or that they were always with me. When I asked my friends if they heard people talking to them who were not there, let's say I got a lot of strange looks. I didn't want to feel different anymore. I didn't want to see those white figures in my room and sometimes the man who would be quietly standing over my bed or in the corner of the room, silently watching me. Sometimes I would see white-bodied figures out of the corners of my eyes; they would disappear as quickly as they arrived. One time I saw an arm and a leg walk right through thin air! I didn't understand who or what it was, and even though I was only 8, I also knew I wasn't crazy; I was a happy kid who wanted a family.

I wanted to live like a normal child. No one else was talking about angels or hearing voices or about the fact that they seemed to know things that no one else did. No one else had dreams which would come true. And this déjà vu thing! I lived with it like it was a daily occurrence. It was a natural progression to say, "No more." And "they" listened, too, meaning the spirit world heard my request! I continued into my teen years experiencing the usual teen girl stuff. My circle of friends began to increase, and I started to really enjoy school. I loved to run and would eventually join the track team. I met my first boyfriend when I was 15. He would be my first love for about four years, seeing me through everything, including the loss of my father. Betrayal and mistrust would soon enter into the relationship. I realize today that this relationship set the tone for many other relationships that would follow. One's first love is more important than some of us realize.

At the age of 15, I also began to experience the journey of migraines, which would continue throughout a good part of my life. This is also around the time when I started to get huge surges of my psychic and medium abilities once again. My feelings about people — the energy that surrounded them — would start to come forward again. I never heard the angels, but this time I started to notice colours. I seemed to see colours around people and things. I was seeing people's auras and beginning to read people and see Spirit again, which wasn't the easiest experience as a teenager.

I was 16 when I began the journey of dreams that kept me up at night. For over six months, I would have one recurring dream every night, which had me waking up terrified and sleeping with the light on. Then one night, my father woke up and looked outside, noticing my bedroom light was on at 1:00 a.m. In the morning, he asked me what was happening. I told him that each night I had a dream in which I was running through the woods and a bear was chasing me. I would call out for him and I would hear, "Your father isn't here to protect you, Marnie. He is in Heaven now. He died. He wasn't well." I would wake up, terrified. He looked at me a little concerned, and of course I asked him, "Are you okay, and are you healthy?" I asked him to go to the doctor and get checked, but he told me he was as healthy as a horse and would live a long time. That isn't what I saw, though. I saw a loving man whose face and skin colour had changed; the light in his eyes diminished as months went on. I would ask myself continually, "Why is no one else seeing this?" The dreams remained until he died from a massive coronary. These dreams were warnings signs from Heaven telling me not all was well with my father. Yet my hands were tied. What could I do? I was only a teenager.

Five years prior, at only 38, he had had his first bypass surgery. I wonder if his heart condition was related to his personal heartaches in life, perhaps even the loss of my mother. I don't think he ever really recovered from the night she took her own life. It was a confusing time for everyone; no one in the family could really understand why she did it.

Sometimes, I would see my dad drift off into deep thought. When I saw him do this, I always saw my mother in my visions. I would ask him if he thought of my mom a lot, and he would smile and say, "Yes, of course I do. I miss her." I would ask if I could get more information about my mom and what happened, but he always told me we would talk about it another time — a time when I was ready. Well, that time never came.

A lesson I have brought into my life is that we truly never know when we are going to pass over into the spirit world, so it's very important to talk about your feelings and emotions now. Don't keep secrets, especially from your children. Tell them what they need to know, when they ask, not when you feel you're ready to talk. I could have really used some answers back then, and I really needed to hear the truth.

Today, with my husband, I never go to bed mad. We take time in the evening to talk about our day and bless our life and our future, and we always kiss our children and each other before we go to bed. I also tell my kids I love them at least three or four times a day!

It's very important to begin your day living in gratitude and thanking the universe and our divine creator (God) for simply being alive and to let people know you love them and care for them!

One of the lessons I have learned over the years is that when we experience a breakup or a loss, everyone experiences some sort of disconnect within the heart. Many times it may feel like your heart is aching. I remember when my father passed, I went to the doctor many times complaining of this pain in my heart and finding out nothing was wrong. What I was feeling was an energy disconnect from my heart chakra to my dad's heart chakra and the stress of this disconnect. When you are sensitive, any kind of pain is maximized, and it can feel like the end of the world.

We are all connected psychically and energetically; the whole world is! Have you ever had an experience in which you thought of a person and he or she called? Or where you seemed to click and knew what the other person was going to say? It's because our thoughts are energy and we connect with others through our chakras — the energy of the mind, body, and soul. Being a healer, when I perform healing on others, I know when they have recently had a breakup or have unresolved grief issues; I can feel it within their heart chakra, and the heart is the doorway to the soul. You will find I refer to this many times throughout this book.

Perhaps if my father had learned to grieve through the losses in his life and heal the heart chakra, he would have had the opportunity to live longer. Even though our births and deaths are predetermined, we do have the ability to live longer if we choose to live healthier; that too is part of our life path. If you can't follow through and do things that will keep you healthy, your soul option may be to die younger. Not everyone is going to have serious health issues within this lifetime, and I also know that many illnesses run in the family. You may have a genetic predisposition to have an illness, and it's up to you to overcome it. Your family may also have health problems due to karmic issues within the family that need to be healed. Just because it is in the family doesn't mean you are going to receive it, however. Your mind is very powerful, and within many spiritual self-help books you will read, "We can heal ourselves by intention."

A couple of days after my father passed away, I would lie awake in my room wondering what the future was to hold and what was going to happen to me, as I had a stepmother who didn't like me. I was only 17 with one more year left until graduation.

I prayed and asked God to show me if everything was going to be okay. As I lay there with the lights on, the room became very cold, and I felt a draft of air pass by me from the left of my bed going to the right towards the window and the wall. As I turned over, I saw my father standing there looking at me. I could only see the upper part of him, and he seemed to look at me like he was standing on the other side of a window. I was, of course, completely shocked, and I felt like I'd had a dose of caffeine; however, back then I didn't know what caffeine felt like, since I didn't start drinking coffee until my late twenties, and today I can't touch it. The next morning, I woke up and realized something wonderful had happened. At that moment, I changed. A realization, an awakening, had happened inside of me that would take years to come out and finally reach the surface.

I never doubted the Afterlife. Remember, my father always said he felt the presence of his dad in our house, and I felt him, too. And many times I would see a white figure that would drift from room to room. Our dog at the time would see it, too. It was the house that once belonged to my father's parents, and my grandfather had already gone into the Afterlife.

When I think back today, a lot of things make sense to me. There were certain places within the house where I felt like someone was in the room with me. I didn't feel afraid, but maybe I felt a little unsure what it was I was experiencing, and when I saw these white figures, I usually stopped what I was doing and watched them float away. Even as I write this, I can't believe I was never afraid. As I passed into my late teens, these white figures would eventually evolve to where I could see more of the physical body, such as the colour of their hair and the clothes they were wearing.

The only time I was completely scared was when my friend and I got a hold of a Ouija board, and I have never touched one since. I was in grade five, and a friend of the family had left a Ouija board in one of the boxes she was storing at our house. No one else was home, so I asked my friend if she wanted to give it a try, and sure enough she was willing. In my room I had two play phones — those phones that operated where one person would go into another room and listen to the other person talk on the phone. They were not plug-in form, just batteries. When we opened the Ouija board up, we asked a question, and though I can't remember the question today, I know I felt very uneasy. We placed our hands on the planchette, and when it began to move, the little phones I had began to ring. My friend and I looked at each other, screamed, and ran out of the house. The phones didn't have any batteries in them! It would take a while for us to go back in, because we were so afraid that something was waiting for us inside the house; but no one was! As for that board, I put it back in the box and told my dad to give it back to its rightful owner.

I do warn everyone who uses divination tools to be very aware of what they do beforehand. Make sure to seek protection for yourself and others, and know that spiritual energy can manipulate objects much easier than any mind or soul. Any divination tool users should ensure the connection is with the right divine source, such as angels and guides that sit closest to God. I learned my lesson that day.

My relationship with my first love would take a turn for the worse after my father's passing. In one argument, he was angry at how our relationship was turning out, as I seemed to need more freedom than he was willing to provide. I needed time to sort things out after my dad's passing. I looked at my boyfriend during that argument and said, "Well, soon you will realize what it is like to not have a father." I told him his father would die soon in a car accident! A couple of months later, his father was out of province and rolled his vehicle. My first love was devastated, shocked, and angry.

I had nothing to do with his father dying. It wasn't even a coincidence; it was simply his time to go, and I was picking up on the energy vibration on what was about to take place or may take place. The sad thing is I had been picking this up more than a year prior to his death. I kept seeing this image when I was around him, and it frightened me. Every time I saw this image, I would call upon God to protect me and everyone involved. I do believe that everything we experience within this life has already been divinely written by the soul self and God. I am grateful for this today; however, back then I didn't understand, and I felt horrible. When my boyfriend told his mother what I had said, she never blamed me; she must have known what I was feeling. In truth, I wanted to run away from life and everything. I was only 17 and felt that my abilities were a curse, and I didn't want any part of it anymore.

My boyfriend would end up moving to another province, which was for the best, and I would continue down the path, looking for love and fulfillment. We were both trying to find ourselves. For some reason, I was also feeling everything everyone else was experiencing too. I had been an empath since childhood, and being an empath can make life very draining when you enter into the world of spirit communication. During my late teens, I began to once again experience glimpses of white figures and even a ghost when I was out one evening. Terrified, I was beginning to think maybe I was going crazy. But still I kept calm, as I never once felt afraid of these spirits and at this time still wasn't hearing any angels. The spirits were not talking to me in the physical form. They were not telling me to do anything, but they were making their presence known to me in a very gentle way.

Being a believer in God and always feeling a spiritual connection to life from a very young age, I began to read the Bible. My birth mother had been a Catholic who prayed with her rosaries daily. I sang in the choir when I was young, and I attended church but not as much as I would have liked to. My stepmother was also Catholic but never seemed to practice its teachings; I had expected her to be filled with more love and kindness. We had this beautiful Bible at home, which we were instructed to be very careful with — and I was. Every time I open that book or when I read the Bible today, I feel so completely relaxed, at ease, and at home. I feel relaxed when I am in graveyards, too!

Remember when I said I wanted to become a nun when I was young? The first people I told were my stepmother and father when I was a teenager. And when I told them, they said *no way*. I was told it would not be a good life for me; I was meant to do something else. It would be years later when I realized that in one of my previous lives, I had been a nun! I have been able to carry that energy with me into this lifetime. What a blessing!

A couple of months after my 18th birthday, I moved out on my own into a bachelorette apartment. With a small inheritance, I diligently worked at my studies to finish grade twelve. It didn't come without a struggle, as I moved to another province to try to finish my final year and to get away from my first love. I missed my friends and my home, so I ended up moving back the following November, which meant I had some catching up to do with my studies. I did pretty well, despite all the upheaval. I bought a used car, furnished and decorated my bachelorette suite, and took some extra courses to make sure I passed grade twelve. I even finished my requirements two months before the deadline. It's amazing what you can accomplish when your drive is focused and you get up in the morning at 5:00 a.m. to study!

The only problem was that all my friends were still in school, so I hooked up with some friends who were a year older and set out to live a life that was pretty much full of partying. It was great at the time! I had just turned 18 years old, and I had no one in sight to tell me what I couldn't do. However, I still felt a tremendous loss; the partying was only suppressing my grief. What I really needed were some good tools to help me move through my grief because I knew my dad wasn't coming back — at least not in the way I was so used to.

I seemed to have many unusual experiences during this time. I would continually see Spirit with my physical eyes. My friends would ask if I was okay. In fact, they often said, "You look like you have just seen a ghost."

I would smile and say, "I'm okay. Just in deep thought about something." During this time, I entered into another relationship, and we really became close, but I still felt something was not quite right. I felt like I wasn't in the right place, that this was not where I was supposed to be. In actuality, it felt like I was living someone else's life. I just existed the best way I knew how and went through the motions of my life, not connected to life or my emotions.

It was later, a year or so after my father's passing, that I would once again see him in spirit. This time, though, it was within a dream; he was talking to me, providing me with some strong guidance — the guidance I needed. I would speak about my dreams to my friends. Some of them would say, "That's wonderful. He is coming through to help you." Others would say, "Marnie, you miss him so much, no wonder you're dreaming of him." I knew better, for these dreams were not normal; they were different. In the dreams, nothing was around us. It would just be him and me, close up and talking. I can still remember everything he said like it was yesterday.

Trying to make sense of my life, having one failed relationship after another, I was faced with my inheritance being almost gone, as I had only enough to help me finish grade twelve and to ensure my needs were being met for a while. Eventually, I needed to rent a room from a friend, as I couldn't afford to live on my own anymore. I worked part-time in retail and on most days nearly starved. I was amazed that I could live off of fries and water for a couple of days. A large bowl of spaghetti would be divided up to last me a week. My grandmother would have been there if I asked, but I didn't; some of my family members seemed to make me feel guilty or made me feel like all of this (my current situation) was my fault. As far as I was concerned, I was on my own, and I would make it on my own no matter what!

I look back now and realize there should have been some support system for me. I was young, grieving, and trying to move forward with what I had learned; yet information about grieving was not available, not like it is today. So I would suppress my grief even more and continue on the best way I knew how.

Just after Christmas, I was laid off work and could not find another job. I felt like a complete loser, to say the least. A friend of the family (my previous babysitter) called me and offered to move me out to Alberta. She would send me enough money for gas and food so I could get out there and live with her. It took some time to really find out if this was something I should do — living back in Alberta. So one evening I prayed and asked for guidance; this time I asked if my father would come through again to help me with this decision. Sure enough, he did. That dream is still so vivid today. He sat me down and said this was the step I needed to take. Maybe one day I could come back and live where I was living, but for now I needed to go and make a life for myself. Then he continued to say that no matter what, he would always be with me. That would be the last time I dreamed of or saw my father in spirit for many years, but his message was so loud and clear; it built a force within me that gave me strength and courage — a feeling that I had not felt before. Even though I hadn't experienced my father within my dreams for so long, I could always sense his presence. He just seemed to stand on the sidelines, cheering me on and ensuring he was not intervening in my life.

There is a rule within the spirit world that your loved ones are never to interfere with your life; they can only discuss items about your life that will help you or guide you. However, they will never tell you to do something that would hurt you or another person or tell you that you don't have options, because you do. When the spirit world is close, you may feel it or see a flicker of light, a bright movement, or a white smoky substance. When you are in silence and all of a sudden think of your loved ones or smell a scent, that's the spirit world trying to communicate with you. Spirits or souls in the Afterlife try desperately to communicate as much as they can. Even though they are busy learning and healing on the other side, they still love you and want you to be happy.

Your loved ones can manipulate electricity by flickering lights or interfering with electrical components in your home. They can also ever-so-slightly move objects; show up as a symbol like a bird, a rabbit, or maybe a butterfly; and even try and speak to you telepathically so that you have a positive memory of them.

There are tons of ways Spirit can communicate with you. It may be different for each individual, because no people are the same, no experiences are the same, and no souls are the same. The meaning or memory the spirit world sends you is always what is significant to you.

I was doing a reading for a young lady whom I will call Alice. Alice wanted to change her career from working in an office to helping animals. Alice had the ability to communicate with animals telepathically, so she was also interested in being an animal communicator, but she was hesitant to do so. It was very clear in the reading that Alice in fact did carry the gift of animal communication. Messages came from her loved ones in Spirit, her spirit guide, and my guide. However, near the end of my reading, she asked me again if this was something she could do — change her career and perhaps communicate with animals on a professional basis. Her loved ones had already told her that she could make this transition and that it would be a successful career move for her. However, she was afraid, and rightfully so; it was a big career move. As soon as Alice asked the question again, the lights flickered on and off in my room. This was Spirit's way of trying to get her attention and reaffirm that all was okay with her choice! Our minds have a tendency to overthink, and our egos try to discredit many parts of our emotional selves, especially our spiritual connections, as the ego is trying to protect us.

Indeed, moving forward and changing her career was a scary task for Alice, and Spirit knew she was going to need all the evidential information it could give her to help her know all was okay with her plans and desires. You will always receive what you need in a reading, just as she did.

When I first met my first husband, I truly believed I loved him, but I was too young to really understand what love was. I was only 21 when we were married. I was really trying hard to find myself, as I had no idea who I was and had no real guidance in my life. The guidance I needed at 21 was reassurance that all was okay, as my self-esteem was so low in those days. Sometimes it felt hard to get up in the morning, but I kept moving forward, knowing someday it would get better.

I would marry my first husband within a year of meeting him and divorce a year and a half later. This marriage would find me living within an abusive relationship. I tried several times to get out but didn't succeed; I was too afraid. There came a day I could no longer take it. My head dented the fridge and the wall of a place we were renting, and I finally said, "Enough!" It was an emotional time, for sure; the marriage seemed to be filled with mistrust and way too much drinking.

If you're a psychic or a medium, alcohol is something you want to minimize or avoid altogether, and you don't want to hang out in bars much either. Not only do nightclubs and places where excessive drinking takes place carry negative energy, but you are also susceptible to picking up a negative energy attachment if you're not careful. This negative energy can come from spirits who have lived before and who are not of the light. This is especially evident if you are visiting a place where lots of angry people hang out or perhaps have died a vicious death and refuse to remain in the light or in Heaven!

These attachments can result in your getting emotionally and physically sick, as alcohol can also interfere with the functioning of your energy field and your chakras, which can then allow you to pick up negative energy that doesn't serve you. Carrying other peoples' energies with you may result in you feeling more tired or depressed, drinking more, or becoming involved in substance abuse and doing things you normally wouldn't do. You are in control of your life, but the energies can try to move you towards a negative path. This means you have to be careful with what you do and who you hang out with when you are a sensitive, empath, psychic, or medium.

Even though I can control my sensitivity, meaning I can minimize my connection with Spirit for a small amount of time, I protect myself constantly and keep my thoughts on love and gratitude as much as I can. I ask Archangel Michael and my spirit guides and angels to protect me from negative energy, too. Your thoughts determine the outcome of your life; awareness is a key factor in remaining within peace. Even today, I do not allow anyone to drink alcohol when I am providing messages from the Afterlife; this is for their safety as well as mine, as any reading can bring up memories of pain and hurt but also of love!

Controlling your connection with Spirit takes a lot of practice, and it is something that needs to be taken care of if you are connecting with Spirit daily. You can do it. I know many people say they can't, but I think it's a must. For myself, if I am in large crowds for more than an hour or so and Spirit starts to come around, my face and entire body seem to become really hot, my heart begins to beat faster, and I become exhausted quite quickly. That's my cue: It's time to go home, or it's time to start delivering messages! Remember, this is my experience; others may have different ones.

Just before my marriage ended with my first husband, we would seek guidance to see if our marriage could last or if we could work out our marital problems. This would lead me to the realization that I needed to find myself and move forward within my own life without him. I was still very young, and I always seemed unhappy and lost in a sense. Yet I always kept looking forward with a sense of knowing that my experiences and feelings were all part of something bigger and much greater. This perception really helped me focus and keep it all together; I needed to surrender and believe there was more to me and to my life than I was currently seeing and experiencing.

The deep desire to help people never left me, and I knew on some level I was destined to work within a helping profession. When I was in my teens, I had thought about being a psychologist when my parents said a firm NO to my desire of becoming a nun. However, given the way the school system was back then (late 1980s) and the fact that I was married, my husband said no when I told him I was going to attend college and told me I instead needed to go get a better job. I was working as a receptionist and disliked every minute of it. When I came home and let him know that I was registering for a four-month course to become a medical office assistant and that this was something I really wanted to do, he only hesitantly agreed. I didn't leave him with a choice, and it should never have been up to him. What one decides to do for a career or education should solely be up to the individual person, in my opinion. You have the answers inside of you; your soul knows what it needs. When someone else starts to dictate your future, that person becomes part of your karma; it may lead both of you on a destructive path!

The course would be 40 hours a week for four months, and 4 to 5 hours a night of study was the norm. I was doing great, though, and was at the top of my class. A sudden appendectomy kept me from class for a couple of weeks, but I was determined to finish the program at all costs. I was able to finish my course with a 99%; I worked hard at it! After my course was finished, I was officially a Certified Medical Office Assistant, and I was so excited and looking forward to my new career. I took a job at a walk-in clinic, and I loved it. I was helping people; it's what I wanted. I seemed to have a knack for relating to all the patients — I really wanted to help them, and I was concerned for them. I started a kind of game with myself, to pass the time: When someone would come through the door, I would try to guess what their issue was before I knew why they were coming in. I was amazed at my own accuracy.

Please note: I think it's important to emphasize that you should never, ever seek a psychic or a medium for medical guidance or a diagnosis. Our loved ones, spirit guides, and angels will provide us with health information, but it's not to be used for medical purposes or as a substitution for medical care. So many times I have had clients come to me and ask why they were not getting pregnant, what was wrong with their heart, or would they die soon, and the list can go on. Can you imagine the predicament a medium or psychic is being placed in with these types of questions? I can assure you, not a good one. Remember, you will always be provided with what is needed within a reading. Sometimes you are not meant to know certain things, so the spirit world will not provide this type of information.

There is an ethic that every person doing psychic or medium work should follow. I have met people who want to be mediums and psychics and feel it's their job to diagnose! If you want a diagnosis for something, please seek the medical assistance of a trained professional. If you want to do medical diagnosing, become a doctor! It's simply that simple.

I have also met my fair share of psychics and mediums who are very quick to say there is a dark force lurking around you and that your company will fail, or you will die soon, and the list can go on. I also have also met those who have brought truth and guidance, and believe me, it's not negative. So be careful when you are seeking guidance from a psychic or medium. Ensure your reading is a good one. Remember, this form of communication is not a joke and should not be used for fun.

I have been told over and over again from my own spirit guides that the only true person to know about death is God. The soul knows when you will die, but it's certainly not up to the medium to tell a person. Now, I am not saying I don't get warning signs, because I do! I received all sorts of warning signs of my father's impending death, of the death of my father's friend, and for my clients. Perhaps if they had taken the warning signs and decided to change their lives towards living better and healthier, their lives could have been prolonged. When a warning sign comes forward regarding health, my clients have already been receiving information because the soul knows, and the body will speak even to its host; yet many individuals either choose to ignore the signs or are simply unaware of these health signs.

That's when a medium comes in handy, since the spirit world will use every opportunity to speak to help another soul in this lifetime. I think this is also why so many psychics or mediums get a bad reputation. They are trying to help people but end up causing more problems for themselves by wanting to prove their abilities (sounds like the ego is trying to take over), which will cause all sorts of frustration for the individual (client) and the medium.

Remember, not all mediums are actually mediums. Seeing a spirit doesn't make you a medium. Connecting with your loved ones in your dreams doesn't make you a medium, either. A medium is someone who can communicate with the dead, and this means providing strong validation and communication with the Afterlife! A medium should be able to provide you with a description of the person and how he or she passed and should be able to bring forward the personality of the deceased. I think the last one is the most important. A medium should also be able to provide you with helpful and loving information from the other side. The deeper the connection with the Afterlife, the deeper the information a medium can provide you with. I also want to mention that no one can become a medium by reading a couple of books, watching some shows, or taking a course over the weekend! It just doesn't work that way.

I always find it difficult when the spirit world provides me with health information. I always let my clients know I am not diagnosing anything! Many times I have been told from the other side that this person needs to see a doctor because he or she is having problems with the throat or glands, only to find out later that this person did indeed have cancer.

If you need to do some healing and get moving forward in your life, Spirit is going to tell you so. But if you are hearing or getting information that you are becoming ill, you will die in a car crash, or your spouse is cheating on you (especially when there has been no indication), your reader may not be dealing with the light; the information may simply be coming from the psychic or medium's own negative beliefs or negative energy. Evil spirits do exist, and they are ready to wreak havoc in your life if you let them. This kind of negative communication can lead the reader to be attached to another person's karma, leaving destruction on both individual's paths.

I think it would be wonderful if in the future the medical or police system would enable the assistance of legitimate mediums and psychics. You never know what the future may bring!

Okay, so back to my first marriage. Even though I loved my job as a medical office assistant, I would once again be led out of this industry due to the lack of funds it would offer. I needed to eat and put a roof over my head, and I seemed to be destined for something more; there was a calling inside me that I could not ignore and yet could not pinpoint.

Everything happens for a reason, and this first marriage was full of first lessons for me. As I began to reflect on my life, my marriage, and me, I noticed something very interesting about myself. I actually was experiencing a lot of physical discomfort during this time. My migraines would come back and increase in strength; these are the same type of headaches I first got when I was 15. It's interesting; these unique headaches that I would get frequently throughout my life would simply go away every time I talked to the other side or did a reading for someone.

I learned, somehow, to deal with these headaches without taking any medications. This is a good thing, as any form of pain reliever seems to numb my senses and make spirit communication difficult. Since my headaches disappear during readings, I have figured out that something may become imbalanced within my energy system when I do not connect with my calling and deliver messages from the Afterlife. I know people can get loaded with psychic energy when they are not grounding themselves after doing psychic and healing work, which can cause all sorts of physical and spiritual problems. If I don't get outside and meditate after doing readings one after another, I can manipulate lights without actually turning them on, and the electronics in my home, including my computer, seem to go a little wonky. The same also happens if I take a break from this work! I'm not sure if this happens to others, but it keeps me in line with my calling and reminds me to make sure I am taking care of myself, too!

THE IMPORTANCE OF SOUL HEALING

When I met my second husband, it felt like a hole that was inside of my soul was being filled from an outside source, which I know today can only lead to destruction. My soul wasn't healed yet, and I didn't know *me* yet. I still required someone else to make me happy, instead of learning how to make myself happy and to value the soul that was within me. Within our second year of dating, he began to become abusive; yet I felt trapped, and the cycle was now beginning to repeat itself. One year before we were to be married, he stopped the abuse until the night before the wedding, when it began once more.

I thought about calling off the wedding, yet I felt so afraid and ashamed about what had happened. I eventually married this man, who would one day leave me on the floor, gasping for air. This experience would guide me to finally feel and hear my guardian angel. Everything has its reason and its lessons; it all depends on how you look at it.

As I have said before, one of the most difficult aspects regarding learning a soul lesson is that if you didn't learn the lesson the first time, it will happen and keep happening until you learn the lesson and have healed from it. The lessons, however, may manifest themselves within different forms, and sometimes it's not your lesson to learn but the other person's, which can make things a little tricky. My lessons manifested in relationships with family, self-acceptance, and self-love.

One could have lessons manifest within health or financial aspects of one's life. All of your lessons can be intertwined, which means they can fall into each other, covering every aspect of your life and leaving the soul in total destruction if healing doesn't occur. This can result in depression and a complete shutdown within the mind, body, and spirit, which may lead the body to experience disease.

Now you may be asking yourself, "Well, if it's part of the plan, won't I experience it anyway?" The answer is yes and no. Every step you take in this life leads you to the next step. Sometimes we need to go down a rocky road in order to find a clear path; you wouldn't have been able to differentiate the clear path if you didn't know what the rocky road was. It's the same idea as knowing light because you know dark or knowing good because you know bad. I consider myself very lucky to be alive today, with some of the soul lessons I have had to learn over the years, and to be able to tell my story and share my experiences.

Abuse should never be put on anyone, no matter what the circumstances are. Anytime someone strikes you, pushes you, shoves you, screams in your face, tries to control you, bullies you, tells you it's your fault all the time, hits you, says you drove them to do it (this is also in the list of infidelity, by the way), or is telling you they can't control their own feelings and emotions, that person is actually telling you, "I need help." It may also mean, "I don't love myself, so I can't love you!"

I can tell you if you are in an abusive relationship and you are afraid that your spouse will hurt you, even when you do get the courage to leave, go and get professional help right away. Go to a place in your area and find a service that helps people within abusive relationships. There is more and more help in this world for people who are abused, and there is an abuse hotline in almost every city in Canada, and I am sure in other countries too. Don't worry about finances or being alone; just get out and find someone who can help you. Everything will work out as it should.

This also goes for anyone who knows someone who is being abused. Please don't tell people you can't be near them or help them if they don't leave their abuser! Also, don't tell them you can't help them because you just can't bear what they are experiencing. That's only going to make them feel more isolated and perhaps cling even tighter to their abuser. They already feel like they don't have any control over their lives. Be a friend. Let them know you are available to them when they need you, and for Heaven's sake, go tell someone this is happening to a person you know, even if it's only to make the police aware of the circumstances. The police will then have their radar on in case someone does call from that home. I know it can be fearful to get into someone else's life, but if we don't try to help people, the perpetrators feel like they have all the control, and they will abuse again.

I have learned from my own experiences that seeking guidance and help shows strength and courage, but many have been brought up to the reverse understanding of this. To them, seeking help is a sign of weakness. I still look back today at what I went through, and it truly feels like it was someone else's life I was living. I am not the same person I was back then, and that helps me realize how successful my healing has been. I can look back with absolutely no negative feelings. I am grateful for the experience. My head and soul are full of knowledge and understanding, and I feel thankful that I am alive today to talk about it.

I remember when my son was 9 months old and I was feeding him at 2:00 in the morning. I heard a scream from outside my living room window. I looked out and this man was bent over a woman who was screaming for someone to help her. I opened up the window and yelled, "Do you need help?"

She said, "Yes, please help me!"

I ran and got the phone and called 911. I went back to the window, and they were gone. I told the police what had just happened. The 911 operator said that if the incident was not happening currently, she needed to let me go, as they were too busy to help. Well, it had happened less than a minute ago! I kept trying to explain to her about this woman who needed help immediately, but the 911 operator just hung up on me. Shocked by my experience, I called the non-emergency line and explained what had just happened, and I was told someone would be sent out to talk to me, but no one ever came. So after I told this story to my family, one of my family members called the local papers, and the story made headlines! I found out later that one week earlier in another province a lady had recently died from a domestic abuse incident where no police were sent when she had called 911. I was asked not to bring this story to the forefront by the police, but I insisted the community needed to be aware of the fault within the system. I just wanted something good to come from this, yet I was fearful for my life; I am not kidding, I was afraid to move forward with this, afraid of putting my family in danger. No one ever threatened me, but I just felt afraid and alone in my quest for telling the truth, and I certainly didn't want the police mad at me for telling my story to the papers!

The end result was that the police services used this phone call situation in their training system describing what *not* to do, and they added more 911 operators. I had to endure the humbling of one of the papers accusing me of not being communicative enough, which was false, as the operator had hung up on me and I only had a couple of seconds to explain the situation. This whole thing became a big ordeal, and I had many hang ups on my home phone over the next week or so, but I was determined to tell the truth of my experience and my story. Women and men need help when their lives are in danger. Shouldn't we all help people instead of being afraid of getting involved? Too many times, I have seen and heard people say they just didn't want to get involved! This was just another learning experience to add to my soul's journey!

If I had only had more help when I was going through the abusive relations, perhaps things would have been easier; but it is and always has been my responsibility to make positive changes with my own life. Now I am not saying a person should become an enabler and just always be there for someone who is experiencing turmoil. Sometimes you need to exhibit some tough love and let that person know you can provide assistance or intervention when needed. The difficulty is that no one can heal if he or she is not ready to do so, no matter how much you try to help.

From my own point of view, I think many women and men stay in abusive relationships because they live on the edge of hope — hope that the spouse or partner will change because they keep saying so without realizing the cycle of abuse. There is a honeymoon stage that usually happens right after an abusive situation. During the honeymoon stage, an abuser may show sincere emotional pain for their wrongdoings and say it won't happen again; they usually begin to say how much they love the person, and then they blame the victim for "making" the abuser act out. Abusers are good at pointing out the flaws of the spouse or partner and showing the victim how they should change to ensure they don't get hit again. I can only tell you from my own situation, but experience has shown me that there is consistency with how the abuser thinks and acts at all times.

Sometimes I think the abuser is so good at lying that they believe their own story, and the victim wants everything to go back to normal and to stay in love. Who wouldn't want to believe everything will be okay? But you can never be sure. I don't believe in "once an abuser, always an abuser"; people can heal if they work hard at it, but it won't happen overnight, and it can't happen without getting some good psychological and spiritual counselling. If all this sounds exhausting to you, you're right — it is!

I can tell you firsthand it is, and sometimes it's so exhausting that the victim has no more energy available to leave the abuser, let alone to see that the abuser is lying. After going through it so many times, a victim's self-esteem is usually so low he or she doesn't know how to move on. This is called the "hot spot," and it's hard to see from the outside world, as abuse in relationships is nearly always a silent killer.

So how can we start the path of awareness and heal our society of this sickness? By bringing domestic abuse out of the shadows! By educating our children on the issue and loving them unconditionally. Lead by example. If you are someone who is abusing a family member, GET HELP! You can bet that the child or person you're abusing is learning something that may either lead them to become an abuser or guide them to learn to be fearful of love. But it doesn't stop there. We need more places for women and men to go to get help and information, and I personally think we need stiffer laws for the abuser, which includes continual psychological help for them.

In order for us to move forward in our lives, we must experience everything our souls have set out to experience before we enter this world. This means the good and the bad. I refer over and over again within this book to the victim state that leaves us stuck within our own perceptions. These perceptions can seem very real to us. We are actually drawing forward experiences that are aligning us within our own belief systems; that is, we will always find what we seek or seek what it is we need to find so our own healing can take place. And society as a whole is not excluded from life lessons; after all, we are all part of society, and we are all interconnected on one level or another.

A SOUL'S WAKE-UP CALL

After I left my second husband, I took a day to think about what I was going to do as I was visiting a family member in another province. I knew I couldn't hide from him; we needed to get a divorce, and I just wanted to make sure this transition would be a peaceful and easy one. However, it was neither.

He wanted everything: the house, the furniture, the vehicle, and the dog! My life became a living hell, to say the least. I don't want to go too much into it, not in this book, as I have already healed from the pain and destruction it brought into my personal and professional life, but I know firsthand that many individuals in our society live in fear daily, waiting and worrying about when their next attack from a loved one will be. That is why I am talking about this in my book. Perhaps my story can help another.

When I did get my life back up and running, I needed to find a job, as I had been recently laid off due to the company closing. I needed to find an apartment to live in, and this was extremely important, as I knew the longer I waited, the more difficult it was going to be to get my personal belongings out of our house. My husband was not a kind or gentle man, and he just wanted to get rid of me so he could go on with his new life, which included a new partner.

As difficult as it was to transition through this breakup, what he did was actually a blessing. I was finally free to start my new journey. By the time I moved into my new place, my second husband had already started dating his new girlfriend — the very one I thought he was having an affair with in the first place. With no money, I settled for what he wanted to give me: a cheque for $1,800 in return for my signature to hand the house over to him. I was shocked and felt like I had just been had. I had put so much of my money and time into building that house. But I wasn't prepared to stay there, and I didn't have the funds available for a long battle with the courts. Besides, he was trying really hard to tell everyone we had ever known that I was completely crazy! I can only imagine what he was saying. It came as no surprise; I was witnessing just another personality trait of an abuser. From my own personal and professional experience, abusers seem to think and try really hard to convince others the person they are abusing is absolutely crazy! Not only have I experienced it myself, but many of my clients have also expressed this happening to them within their own relationships. I think abusers feel it gives them an edge or provides an alibi for what they have done.

By this time I couldn't physically or emotionally handle much more stress, and I didn't want my life to be in financial ruin, either. Taking this small amount of money allowed freedom into my life along with a feeling of safety. He left me alone after I agreed to his terms. I don't recommend this route for everyone, but I really had no choice at the time. I couldn't get any legal assistance, as I had no money for a deposit with a lawyer. Most of all, I had no more fight within me; I was exhausted. I wanted to be free of the life I had with him. I have no regrets about what I did, as money is money. He will need to live with his soul and his memories forever, and his girlfriend will, too.

It's interesting that one of our biggest fights near the end of our marriage was about him and a woman he worked with. She was a couple of years younger than me and was always calling him at home, all the time. I felt at this time that he had completely withdrawn from our marriage.

My guides kept telling me he was having an affair, and I felt like he was, too! When I finally left him, and before we made any agreements, I got a sudden urge to go to a specific restaurant, one that I had never been to before. I couldn't explain to my friend this need or urgency, but I needed to go to this specific restaurant at a specific time. When we arrived, I knew instinctually which table to sit at, and as we sat down and had a drink, she and her boyfriend asked why I had picked this place. I said that I didn't know but that something was going to happen that I needed to see. I got the strangest look from my friends.

Within an hour the energies started to shift around me. I looked at the front door, and lo and behold, my husband came walking in, holding hands with the woman he worked with. My friends were in shock and couldn't believe their eyes. Spirit had shown me once again that what I had were true feelings. I wasn't crazy like my ex tried to tell me and everyone else, over and over again. He was caught red-handed. I had my final victory!

After this incident, when I had been working a couple of months, I decided to rent a small apartment. It wasn't in the best shape, but it was mine. When my closest friend at the time and her boyfriend helped me move in, they asked if I wanted them to stay and unpack. I looked at them and said thanks for the offer, but this was something I needed to do on my own. After they left, I closed the windows, unplugged the phone, turned on the TV, drank pop, and ate pizza and any junk food I could get my hands on. I cried all weekend with sheer joy! I felt safe, and I felt excited for the unknown. I knew this journey was not going to be easy, but I felt fulfilled and happy, which were emotions I hadn't felt for a very, very long time.

In the following years, I was trying to climb the ladder in business, working for different companies and desperately trying to find myself. This was my time — a time to rediscover Marnie. I went on the journey of learning meditation, which led me to self-development and spiritual self-help books. I really began to look within myself. When I started to learn how to silence my mind, old thoughts and emotions began to resurface. I had spent more than ten years trying to keep them buried. I had wanted and needed to suppress my pain. I think it was the only way I could survive everything that was happening to me at the time.

I didn't have much education at the time, and I had to work really hard to get my life back on track, financially, spiritually, and emotionally. I continued for more than fifteen years working myself up in the corporate world. I became really good at sales, as I always knew exactly what kind of person I was dealing with. During this time, this "knowing" seemed to increase, and I began to know what was going to happen with specific people. I was working as a Recruitment Specialist for an employment recruiting firm at one point. My boss felt I caught on to the job way too easily and quickly. This seemed to bother her. I, on the other hand, enjoyed the job immensely and was confused by her remark that perhaps I had already done this work with another company. I think she thought I had lied on my employment application and in fact had worked within this type of position before. But I never did, so I eventually left the company, feeling uncomfortable with these comments. I was a natural in employment recruiting; my skills in interviewing and placement seemed impeccable. I could always make a good match for the employee and the employer. I would get phone calls from both parties thanking me for placing the client or providing the employee with such a wonderful opportunity.

When I began to heal, I learned to trust my instincts, and believe me, intuition can help a person with his or her career; it helped me tremendously with mine. However, one of the most important lessons I needed to take away from this specific job was to realize the importance of listening to my intuition within my professional life. I had to realize that not everyone can connect or believe in his or her own intuition or the importance of it, and I was to learn to be okay with that realization.

This would be the job that would change many things for me. I began getting heart palpitations, and my blood pressure would begin to rise. I was only 31! How could this be? After visiting a neurologist for my dizzy spells, he said perhaps this might be a good time for a career change, as every time I spoke about my work, I developed read patches around my neck and face, which was an indication of stress. However, finding a new career was a lot easier said than done. So this too began to cause me a lot of stress. I went on to find a less stressful job, only to begin feeling less valued and more frustrated. I took a more administrative role with less pay, and financially I still wasn't doing very well. I had a lot of work to do in the financial realm to get back what I had lost through my divorce.

Working and living in the city cost quite a lot. I sold my car and moved closer to my job downtown. It took me only ten minutes to walk to work, so it was a sacrifice I could live with. I loved to ride my bike and was lucky to have a pathway that was only minutes away from my apartment.

With all that had already taken place in my life, I still felt disconnected, and I wasn't very happy. During my time for me, I had come to terms that for years — ever since I could remember — I had literally no self-esteem. I was always trying to heal and pick myself up constantly; it was hard, and on most days I had no support group — or so I thought.

It always felt like people didn't get me, and yes, at times I was still shy. I always felt different, and when people asked me about my life before, I was embarrassed to talk about it. Can you imagine trying to explain to someone you met that you are not crazy! *I have been divorced twice, both had been abusive relationships, my mother committed suicide when I was 7, and I have been on my own since I was 17. Oh yeah, I think my angels talk to me, and I seem to know things about life and people that others don't see. I can talk to dead people, and I see ghosts ...* I think any normal or perhaps unaware person would run for the hills!

Keep in mind; this was my perception at the time — a perception that was coming from a place of fear, unworthiness, and unawareness. My exes did a good job of making me feel small, and I did a good job of believing them!

My value system concerning myself was pretty much deep in the toilet, and I had not yet learned about how our thoughts, emotions, and perceptions create our reality, which creates our lives. No, I felt like a victim — but I was a victim who was healing and one who desperately wanted a better life for herself, and I was going to do everything within my power to make sure I lived life to its fullest and survived. Realizing this was my first step in healing and personal growth.

All I had experienced was allowing me to get more in touch with my intuition. Intuition is a vital component of survival and personal growth. We all get that sense that something isn't right, or we think we should have turned left instead of right; it leaves you saying, "I knew I should have done that," or "I knew I should have said that." Your intuition is here to help you, but it's hard to listen to it if you have no self-esteem and if you always doubt yourself. Other people may have taught you for years that the feelings you are experiencing are not real, because you're too sensitive. I have learned over the years that many individuals who are naturally sensitive seem to have a high degree of doubt about their own intuition from an early age.

This is a learned behavior that most likely has been reinforced by someone they love. It's a scary thing to think that you are a powerful person who has the ability to control the outcome of your own life. Sometimes it's easier to listen to others than to understand intuition, and many find it a lot easier to blame others for their mistakes than to make the conscious effort and listen to their own intuition. Intuition can also be called hearing the God within, your higher power, the higher mind, and the super-self. The fact is that intuition is part of your DNA and was given to you by God to help you move through the difficult times. There will be more on intuition later in the book.

I knew it was going to take some time and a lot of hard work on my part — a lot of letting go, reading self-help books, healing the past, and getting the courage up to see myself and my life in a much different light — so I went to the library and got busy reading. I completely submerged myself in this for about a year. I got enough courage and registered myself in college, and I started to work in the evenings towards my psychology degree.

I tell you this was extremely powerful and difficult for me at the same time. I had to learn how to learn all over again, as it had been many years since I had done that kind of educational work. It was comforting to know that I wasn't alone; there were many older people in the class alongside me.

I had tried to go into social work when I met my second husband; it didn't last for long. I was weak and listened to someone else's advice, but eventually I stepped into the threshold of my own power and began the journey of higher education, and my grades were great!

During this time I read more self-help books. I became an avid reader of the Bible and anything Anthony Robbins wrote. I truly believe his insights changed my life. When I read the book *Awaken the Giant Within*, I felt like his writings were saving my life. When I picked the book up and looked at the back, it said to wake up and take control of your life! That pretty much summed up exactly what I needed to do. One of the quotes in his book says, "'Experience is not what happens to a man; it is what a man does with what happens to him.' —Aldous Huxley"

This quote reminds me time and time again that our souls are on this planet for one purpose: to experience. If we take an experience and turn it into gratitude, we can see the lesson and use the experience to help someone else. It is that simple.

Even though I experienced some difficult times, I can say today that it was my decision to experience what I had to experience. Now this doesn't mean that what others had done was right; it wasn't. No one should ever hit another human being. No one should ever cause someone else fear or try to control someone's life, under any circumstances. However, it is my responsibility to take initiative in my life and learn how to better it. That can be difficult at times. Keep in mind that even though I write this in 2014, these events took place in my life in the 1990s.

We have come a long way in helping women and men get out of abusive relationships and heal. Education on this topic is more available these days, and you can find a self-help book on just about every shelf in every bookstore and library.

I think one of the most valuable tools in healing is taking initiative on those intuitive hits you get. Listen to your internal guidance. If something doesn't feel right about a person or about the career you're in, you're probably right: Something isn't right for you. It doesn't mean something is not right *with* you! The career or the person may seem great to everyone else, but if it isn't right for you, it's not meant for you. Something better is waiting for you, and it won't reach you unless you embrace the steps that take you where you need to go.

One Saturday, I woke up and felt some strange energy shifting around me. Spirit was near; I could feel it. All of a sudden, I got the idea that today I was going to the library. So I hopped on the train and headed to the library. As I was on the train, I realized I had no idea why I was going to the library! I just knew I had to go. So as I walked into the building, I stood right in the middle of the front doorway and felt I needed to head over to the personal development area, not knowing why or what I was to find. I trusted my knowing. I felt drawn to a location, and as I bent down a book fell off the shelf, which I caught; the book was called *Spirit* something — I think it was *wellness*, but I am not positive. I do know that when I named my company, my guides brought me back to the memory, and I named my company Spirit Wellness Inc., as this book changed my life and brought me back on my spiritual and intuitive path. Again, I can't express the importance of listening to the intuitive hits you can get on a daily basis. I am not sure how much longer it would have taken me to move forward with my healing if I had not listened to my intuition and headed off to the library. Spirit works in interesting ways and is always trying to send us messages. We just have to listen!

As I have learned over the years, you need to be aware of your surroundings if you want to hear or see the messages from the other side. Imagine trying to connect with someone when there is a glass wall situated between you. You may try to flick the light switch to get your loved one's attention, blow wind around that person's face so he or she can feel or sense your energy, or leave coins or place things in the wrong areas just to get that person's attention. Yet that person still may not respond. Well, this is just like the world of spirit. Communication is all around you; you just need to listen and keep your eyes open.

Before I got the book from the library, I was already well on my way in meditating and working with spiritual manifesting, and it worked extremely well. I would tell the universe what I needed and how I was going to get it, and it worked! I was able to manifest a car and a new job; my life was heading in the right direction, my self-esteem increased, and I finally began to learn about myself. For the first time in a long time, I felt safe and complete in my own skin. It wasn't an easy road, but I would have to say that after I started to learn that I wasn't so different after all and that there were many people in this world who experienced what I experienced, this brought forward a sense of peace. I began to become my authentic self. I started to work with affirmations. I looked at myself in the mirror daily and said what I believed. "I am a loving, happy, wonderful person who has so much to give and offer this world." So once I started to feel good about myself again and after I got the junk out of my life, it was time to meet the perfect man.

However, this time it wasn't so clear. I was still single and trying to manifest my perfect man, who would arrive one day. Yet I still kept meeting men in my life who didn't seem to fit me! I guess it was the dating process, or I was supposed to learn something from meeting the wrong people. I felt good, and I was ready — or so I thought! I revisited myself in meditation to find out that I still had some old wounds to heal and that I needed to forgive everyone in my life. So I did the best I could with what I had at the time.

I would visit a psychic to get some answers. This would be the second time I had ever visited one, but the calling to do so was extremely overpowering, and I couldn't ignore it. So I went to the farmers' market one day. I saw a sign that said "Psychic Readings," and as I walked closer, I hesitated. The area where she was doing her readings looked dark and kind of scary. There were black curtains wrapped around where she was sitting, a small light, and pictures of some stars. It just didn't seem very welcoming, almost like I was stepping into a dark dungeon or some sort of lair! I didn't have anything to lose, though, so I said to myself, "What the heck, why not?"

As I sat down, she gave me this strange look. I was so nervous, I didn't even know what to say or ask! She did my reading and was completely correct with some of my past experiences and my current situation. She looked at me, oh so very closely. "Do you know you are a psychic and a medium?" Then her eyes got really big. "You're even more psychic than me!"

I lowered my head and replied, "Well, I have always felt a little different, and I seem to know things that others may not know. I also feel my deceased father when he is around. I have seen him, and I also smell his cologne. I have seen other spirits many times from the age of 5. I hear little whispers from time to time, guiding me or letting me know that I'm not alone. I never really feel alone, as I always feel this presence of beautiful energy around me."

She looked at me in amazement. "Girl," she said, "you have to learn how to enhance this ability, as you have an incredible future ahead of you!" I wanted to run away so fast, but I kept listening. Then she asked if I was pregnant.

"No," I said, "not unless I'm the Virgin Mary." She chuckled and continued with the reading.

I went back home and began to cry. I felt more confused than ever because I didn't want that kind of life. What would people think of me if I told them I could talk to the dead? I didn't say anything to anyone, as I was sure everyone would think I had lost it. So yes, I still had the fear that people would think I would do the same thing my mother did. It was a fear that would take me more than ten years to face and clear. There were lots of deep wounds that needed healing, because Band-Aids can't last forever. As far as being pregnant, I didn't think that would ever happen, but I did think that having a baby with my second husband would have somehow made our life easier. It wouldn't have, and besides, we found out both he and I would have had difficulty conceiving due to infertility issues with both of us.

I had been attending university in the evenings for about three years, preparing in my training to become a psychologist, so I thought, yes, one day my life would change for the better. After all I had been through, I was finally getting some education in a field that I was sure I would love, and if I couldn't have children, I was okay with that. I was still feeling hopeful!

At no time did I ever feel that I was in some way veering into the dark side or that I was doing something that God did not want me to do. Everything I was doing was all for bettering my life and my future. Please note that this manifestation of furthering my education and the positive feelings about my new path were there because I was in alignment to receive these things. Things don't just happen; people don't just show up because you ask your guides and angels to do so. Life doesn't work that way. You need to be ready to receive. God never gives you more than you can handle. It's another universal truth in the Law of Attraction. My healing was bringing me into alignment to receive. I had the thoughts or the desires I had because my soul and my intuition were telling me that I was on the right path and that I had done some serious spiritual movement within my life. The Afterlife and my higher self were guiding me so I could receive information that was needed for my current path and for my future. Spirit is always sending us signs and messages.

Still, to this day, I am receiving messages daily from Spirit. A couple of months prior to this writing, I would continuously see hearts. Hearts were in the sky. I took a hot pot off the stove and put it on a glass cutting board, then lifted it up, and the moisture from the pot formed a perfect heart. The snow was melting around our tree one day, and it melted into a shape of a heart. My son woke up on Valentine's Day, and his eczema had flared up and took a shape of a heart! I told him he was marked by the angels. God was telling him how much he loved him. One day while I took my kids for a walk, I was looking down at the ground, and lo and behold I saw a heart on the road; it looked like some kind of moisture mark, yet there was no rain in sight! These moments provided reassurance and love, and they put a big smile on my face!

Even before I went through the motions of healing, I had always known love was a fundamental part of life and our growth. After I put everything the psychic told me into perspective, I felt completely ready — more ready than I ever had been — to move forward within my life and to find true love. I was set up on a blind date from a friend. I talked to the man who is my husband today, and we made arrangements to meet for coffee.

The next day I was so excited and also a little nervous. Just listening to our conversation over the phone and his voice, I knew it was going to be a great night. I arrived at the restaurant first, and as he came in, I stood up and shook his hand. Within a second, I saw my life pass before my eyes. I saw a baby boy who looked exactly like our son today and our marriage, and I viewed us being happy and in love. I was a little taken back at all the images I saw within my mind, as this had never happened to me before. I tried very hard to keep an open mind, be objective, and make sure this was in fact something that was real.

Within a couple of minutes of his arrival, we sat down and talked. We talked for hours. I had never felt so comfortable with someone, so at ease. It was like I had found an old friend. Everything about him seemed so familiar. I kept telling everyone that I had found my second half, not really knowing at that time what it meant. I felt like I had found the other part of me. After a couple months of dating, he asked me to move in, and within one year we were engaged. Two months after announcing our engagement, I found out I was pregnant! No, I couldn't believe it myself. I wasn't sure if I could ever have children. My fiancé was aware of it and okay with it. I had hoped I would be able to have at least one child, one day.

The morning I found out I was pregnant, I didn't know if I should laugh, cry, or scream! I was terrified of giving birth, and I was in shock. Of course it all worked out well. It was interesting — the week prior to finding out I was pregnant, I had been extremely tired. I went to bed every night at 7:00 p.m., slept straight through, and woke up at 7:00 a.m. My fiancé would tell me I was sleeping like a rock. As I write this, I now know the number 7 is also the number of creation. It would be a difficult pregnancy and delivery; I knew we would have a boy with dark hair and dark eyes, just like the images I had seen when I shook my fiancé's hand when we first met, and voila! It was a little baby boy, who was medium skinned with dark hair and dark eyes; he looked exactly as I had seen him in my inner visions. He took after my side of the family! I wanted to do something different after my son was born. I had a huge urge to get him baptized. Even though I was never baptized, nor was my husband, it seemed like it was the right thing to do — and I knew my husband and I were next.

While still going to school part-time in order to finish my psychology degree and working full-time, I became pregnant with my second child. It was a great pregnancy. We moved out of the townhouse we were in and into a small home. We would stay only a year there; Spirit was trying to push me forward.

It was after this pregnancy that much would change in my life. I almost lost my second son; he had a difficult time keeping anything down, constantly choking on my milk and the formula I would give him. The doctor told me this can sometimes happen to a newborn, He wasn't sick, and there was no indication of any structural abnormalities. I would have to sleep with him and keep my eyes on him every moment of the day. The minute I felt or saw him start to choke, I would reach over and grab him. I often thought if I weren't there, he would choke to death. I was a bit of a wreck, scared and feeling very alone, as this went on for the first six to eight months of his life. There wasn't much help for me. I grew used to it. I had been pretty much on my own, it felt like, most of my life, so I knew one day I would bounce back. This was the year when my mother in spirit made her presence very well known; she was constantly on my mind, and I felt like I was being guided into all sorts of different directions. These directions would allow me to achieve further healing.

As my son began to strengthen, so did I. It was time for all of us to get baptized. What a wonderful time. When the moment arose and I was being baptized, I had this huge amount of release come over me. It felt like a huge block was being taken off my shoulders, and I just wanted to flop to the floor and cry after the ceremony, but I didn't! There were too many people attending and watching, and after all, I didn't want to come across as dramatic!

The days that were leading up to this baptism seemed to be so tense for some reason. I wanted everything to be perfect, for all of us. Once the baptism was done, we came home and celebrated. That evening was the first time we finally all slept through the night, and something powerful changed and shifted deep within my soul.

One day just after the baptism, my husband and I were in our room with the new baby, and we heard our first son talking in his room. A little confused by this, I crept into the hallway to listen. It sounded like he was talking to someone in his room. My son was 3, and was carrying on a good conversation with someone! I opened up the door, and he had this bright smile on his face. He looked at me, then looked back into thin air and said, "Oh no, Mommy. He is gone."

I asked, "Who is gone?"

He said, "Grandpa."

I had never shown my son the picture of my family or my father, as everything was still packed away. I asked him, "What did this man say to you?"

My son told me, "He said he was my grandpa, your dad, and he was sorry that he wasn't able to be here with me. He told me he would have loved to take me fishing, because he loves to fish, and he told me you would never take me fishing and that he didn't know why. He said he loved the mountains and the trees and wished he could go hunting with me when I was older."

I was shocked, to say the least, as my son was explaining my father exactly as he had been when he was alive! I went downstairs and dug up the pictures and brought one to my son. The picture I showed him had several people in it, and I asked him to point to the man in the picture — the one he had been talking to. He pointed directly to my father in the picture. I felt so happy and excited that my son was given the opportunity to meet his grandfather. This visitation would be followed with many more spiritual happenings.

It was at this moment that I took a serious look at my life once again. I desperately had a desire to go back to where I grew up and have my children grow up in the same small town. I had the desire, more than ever, to go back and try to find out what had happened with my mother. The feelings became so strong I could no longer ignore them. My husband had grown up close to where I used to live, and he had always wanted to go back to that province too.

It was in 2005 when the economy hit an all-time high; house prices literally increased by 50%. The time had come to sell and move on. Our home sold in less than 24 hours, and in one month we were off to a small town in British Columbia (home).

We found a duplex up in the mountains; it was a dream! I would look out my window and see the peaks. It needed some work-through, but I was ready! I started to renovate, take care of the boys, and reopen the old chapters in my life. I got reacquainted with some old friends, and everything was going pretty well. It was about six months into living in our new residence when the urge to get moving forward to find information about my mother resurfaced. I felt like I didn't have much time; Spirit was telling me to get a move on. Time was of the essence.

One morning I woke up and spoke to my husband. "Let's get ready. We are driving to the small town where I grew up!"

He looked at me and said, "Marnie, that's two hours away."

I said, "I know, so let's get moving, or we will be late."

"Late for what?"

"I don't know. We have to get a move on, and we have to arrive by 12:00 to have our lunch."

He put a smile on his face and said, "Okay!" As we started to drive, I explained to him that something was waiting for me in this small town and I needed to go today; there was urgency to my feelings. This was the place where my mother had ended her life more than thirty years before. We finally arrived! It was really a small place with only one gas station, a corner store, and a small restaurant. We stopped in the restaurant to have some lunch.

As we sat down, I looked around and saw lots of old pictures. My husband asked if I recognized anyone. I said no. As I looked over to the left, I couldn't help but notice a woman staring at me; she really never stopped staring at me. As we finished our lunch, she came over and asked my name — actually, my maiden name. Her eyes grew big, and she said, "I knew it! I knew you when you were young. I knew your mom and dad." In fact, she owned the restaurant. She also told me she didn't eat there often, but today she had. She had felt this urgency to come here at this time. It was divine intervention; it had to have been. She gave me some names of people I could talk to, and the investigation was on.

I desperately wanted to find my mother's ashes and have a memorial plaque for her. This venture was so important to my own healing and growth. I felt like every step I took was bringing me closer and closer to healing the past. But I didn't know where to look. My father and mother had been married; they had seemed happy at the time but also spoke about divorce close to her passing. Some days I could feel there was a lot of friction between them. Remember — shortly after my mother passed away, my father would become engaged to our babysitter, and then he married someone else. There didn't seem "enough time" to talk about my mother, her passing, or even her funeral. My father died before I could really get any clear information about her suicide. I just had my memories, and they were still very clear and vivid. I wasn't receiving a lot of information or help from the small family I did contact, as some of them just didn't remember a lot about those days.

So I did the best I could and would finally decide to put my mother's memorial plaque right beside my father's. She would be happy then. I felt like a chapter had finally closed, yet I was physically, emotionally, and spiritually exhausted over the whole ordeal. My body was finally saying, "It's time to relax," but I wasn't listening. Your body is always talking to you, and you have the choice to listen or to not. Feeling a little stressed from life itself and overcoming a difficult cold, I was ready for the hills! So my husband and I went out skiing!

When we finished lunch, I began to feel a little dizzy. As we headed up the mountain on the chair lift, I looked at my husband and said I wasn't feeling very well. He said I looked a little pale. As we got off the chair, I looked at him and said I couldn't breathe! Stars were all around me, my heart was pounding, and I thought I was going to die! Being stubborn as I was, I headed down the mountain one step at a time and repeated to myself that under no circumstance was I going to die on this mountain! We headed straight for the hospital.

With no idea why I was having heart palpitations, dizziness, and chest pain, I was kept in the hospital overnight for observation. That night my life would once again change. I remember lying in the hospital bed. I could barely sleep because the man next to me was snoring so loudly, so I had a lot of time to look over my life, and the only thing I could think about was my husband and kids. I couldn't imagine not taking care of them; our kids were only 2 and 5. I told myself that I was going to take better care of myself, start living less stressed, and be happier. The doctors let me go the next day and gave me some medication, but I was to see a heart specialist in a couple of weeks. They did say if I felt that way again to come back. That evening at home as I was lying in bed, I started to get pains again, and in trying not to panic, I prayed and prayed.

I remember saying, "God, please let me live. Please let me see my children grow old. God, I promise from this day forward I will follow any path that you place before me. Please show me what it is you want me to do, and I will do it. Please let me be okay."

At that moment I felt a beautiful energy surround me; it was so warm and relaxing, and I knew everything would once again be okay. My guardian angel's wings had wrapped around me once more. The next morning, I looked at my husband and said, "I'm sure I will be okay, but I am not the same woman that was on that hill the other day." He looked at me, seeming a little confused, and asked me to explain. Well, I couldn't. "My life will change, and I have changed. I'm going to be the best wife and mother anyone could ever have." He said I already was!

I got a clean bill of health from the doctor's office. My mother's memorial plaque was all set and ready to go, and I was feeling better having made some huge decisions about my career. I had been working so hard and for so long, trying to finish my degree, but I knew I had to start doing something different now! I needed to find a way to start helping people now, so there was no time to waste. I prayed to God, and I knew that he would show me what I needed to know when I was ready.

It was a month later that my husband and I knew it was time to move again. Even though we loved our house and it had been renovated perfectly for us, it did have a lot of strange happenings in it!

The kids and I heard a male voice one morning. It came from the basement close to the room where the master bedroom was. When this happened, the kids would jump! The phones would ring nonstop, too. I actually called the telephone company on numerous occasions, complaining that something was wrong with our phones. We would go out for a couple of hours and come back to find all the phones ringing at once inside the house. I had even bought three sets of new phones. I suppose we were never meant to stay long. It would take us into the fall to sell our home, but we did it, and we were back living in Alberta by November. I started my schooling again and worked part-time so I could take care of my boys. Once we moved, I began to have panic attacks. This was something I had never had before, and I felt miserable. However, the panic attacks had nothing to do with the move; they were another lesson on my soul's journey of learning and experiencing.

I knew I wanted to get working within the helping profession sooner than later. I didn't know what to do with my career, and I had pain within my body that was undiagnosed. I kept getting strange sensations throughout my body. I began to see and hear Spirit again; everything seemed so intensified, stronger than ever before. So I decided I would meditate, and I said out loud, "Okay, God, you need to tell me what my next step is, and I'm not leaving this room until I hear it!"

To my surprise — the answer would take 30 minutes or so — I heard the word *Reiki*. I had no idea what the word was, and when I Googled it I couldn't find anything. I tried Googling it again, and some information came up regarding Reiki. I read with much enthusiasm, having no prior information about this topic, but it sounded really interesting. So I signed up for all three courses at the local college, and I felt I was ready for something!

ENERGY HEALING FOR THE SOUL

T he morning I arrived at the Reiki course was chaotic, to say the least. I was stressed beyond limits, my nose would not stop running, and I thought for sure I was going to be sick. I had already paid for the course, and I knew this was something I needed to do. I must have looked and acted like a wreck! In fact, I think I was a wreck! Little did I know that my soul and the spirit world had set me up for something great!

I seemed pretty much in a daze but couldn't keep my eyes off the instructor. I listened to every word she said. I was amazed at what she was telling me; this was so cool, I thought! After my first attunement, I felt so different and relaxed as well. There would be one month of cleansing until my next attunement, and I read as much as I could in the interim. It would be in the second course that I would experience how my own abilities could help another person. The instructor kept mentioning my "gifts" — the fact that I could smell, feel, see, and hear the spirit world was a gift from the creator. *Okay,* I thought, *what now?*

I would do some heavy releasing in the second level. In fact, I did a lot of releasing about my past experiences. These experiences included my divorce and the deaths of my mother and father. I began to read almost every spiritual self-help book out there. There were be two books that would start me on my spiritual journey: *You Can Heal Your Life* by Louise Hay and *Healing with the Angels* by Doreen Virtue. I began doing Reiki healing for my husband and my children, and I was amazed at the information I was receiving for them. It was after my third attunement that I started to actually understand what it was I was truly experiencing.

My experiences were exciting and fearful all at the same time. I finally realized the depth of my abilities, and as I began to embrace these "gifts," I began to feel more and more complete.

My first actual medium reading was done within one of my Reiki healings. I say this because even though I had been receiving and providing messages all my life, I had actually never set the intention to do it. I also want to be clear that a medium reading should not be done within a Reiki healing session. Mediumship is validating life after death, and within Reiki healing, the Reiki practitioner should be relaxed, or it's not beneficial to the client. How are you going to provide validation to the client when the client is perhaps sleeping?

I had seen spirits before — heard them, felt them — and I had seen my father with my physical eyes. This time, though, I was seeing spirits for someone else, in a very different way. I was amazed and still very cautious. My family was cautious, too! My husband watched with anticipation and some apprehension of this skill his wife had immersed herself in. He had always known I was a little different but didn't really know what I was going to do with my gift.

Years prior to this moment, I had been reading *Law of Attraction* and other self-help books, so I knew I was on a huge journey of clearing and growth, but it on a completely different level from my previous healing. It seemed like divine intervention was continually stepping in. I was in a class and several ladies there had unique experiences; many of them had their own clearing that they were going through. The class was truly an empowering experience.

My husband, who was my first real Reiki client, was ready to experience energy healing. He needed a lot of energy replacement where he had had surgery after his car crash. As I was doing the Reiki session, I noticed how everything in the room and within me became very cold. However, my husband fell right into a deep sleep; his healing had begun! As I went over the scar on his back, an image of a man came through. The energy was thick and very difficult to maneuver, and I knew I was dealing with a thought form and some residual spiritual energy that wasn't happy. My husband was still fast asleep and wasn't able to feel any of this. I immediately went into a prayer and put the Reiki symbols over his scar and asked Archangel Raphael and Archangel Michael to help me remove this negative energy. I replaced this energy with their beautiful white light to help my husband heal from this tragedy. At the same time, I also asked that the entity or the negative energy that was remaining here be released. I called my guides and angels in to help with that and send it back where it came from with love; this helped this energy form cross over into the light.

For someone one who was a newly trained Reiki Master, I certainly learned quickly about the power of prayer and angelic help and guidance. I was literally the facilitator on this healing journey. The spiritual energy that was surrounding us was intense and beautiful. Of course, after I finished the healing, I woke my husband up and asked, "Well, how you did like it?" He said of course it was great; he felt so relaxed, and his lower back pain was gone! With a smile I said, yes, that's where the angels and I had worked the most on! I was exhausted, but he was relaxed!

After doing Reiki for a couple of months, I felt that I still needed to learn more, but I had no idea what "more" there was. I saw tons of advertisements about courses, but none of them intrigued me until I saw an ad titled "Angelic Healing Practitioner Course." My heart jumped, and I knew this was the next step. I took the course and learned all about angelic healing and angel readings. I couldn't believe all the angels that were available to us. I knew my guardian angels intervened in my life on numerous occasions, and I had always believed in them. It was during this course that I began to wake up to even more knowledge!

I took all three levels of the angelic healing course and knew I was ready for more. I became more and more comfortable with my skills. I was surrounded by people who accepted me and helped me realize this was all part of my divine path.

My angels and guides had been preparing me from the age of 5, if not earlier. I knew I had always been psychic, as well as a medium who could see things that other people didn't, but it would take until now to realize what I could do with these gifts and how much control and power I had over my own life! Every step of this journey seemed to be completely guided by a higher power.

One morning I woke up and said to my husband, "It's time to open up my company." He looked a little unsure of what would lay ahead for me. I told him not to worry, because I had a plan! A couple of days later, I got an urge to go and register my company as an incorporated company, and I knew I needed to do it immediately, not tomorrow. So I pulled out the yellow pages and found the nearest registry office. I called and said I wanted to incorporate a company and needed to find out the process. I was down in their office signing papers in less than two hours. The name I chose was Spirit Wellness Inc. I was so excited. The emotions that were pouring through me were incredible. I felt like I had given birth to something incredible. I would start my journey by doing Reiki Healing and Angel Readings. The enthusiasm came from friends I had met within my workshops and from my husband. My children were excited too! They wanted to learn what I was learning. I also think they saw and felt how happy Mommy was, and they knew this was a positive thing; remember, all kids are intuitive.

It wasn't all roses, though. I came into many challenges — challenges I would have to face if I wanted to keep going on this journey. When I first had my website developed, I wanted to let all our family members know so they would be the first ones with the opportunity to view it. You can imagine how nervous I was, after all I spent years trying to be normal and not to let anyone think I might turn out like my mom. Their reply? "That's nice, Marnie." Then some of them secretly had a discussion, thinking I had completely fallen off my rocker — after all, I was talking to angels! And being a healing conduit for spiritual energy! What was that all about? I would realize later that educating people is first and foremost. Once they have all their information, then they can place their opinion; it doesn't mean they are correct, though. After all, Doreen Virtue had her Ph.D. and was training people all over the world! I had to remember that had I agreed to have these individuals in my life when I began the journey long, long ago. Their reaction only gave me strength!

Months later, it didn't matter anymore, as I would see incredible healing take place and messages would come through that would change people's lives for the better. You can't imagine how I felt; I was finally doing something I loved: helping people! The journey wasn't over yet; Spirit had something else in mind!

So what is Reiki anyway? *Reiki* is a Japanese word meaning "universal life force." It's a form of energy healing that is performed by gently placing your hands over another person, allowing the flow of energy from practitioner to client. While it's extremely powerful, it's equally as gentle and can be channeled by intention; that is, the practitioner can send healing energy through space and time for another person. Reiki is also called *distance healing*.

Reiki is a spiritual art of healing that gently balances life energies, bringing health and well-being to your clients and also to yourself. When the flow of life force energy is disrupted or weakened, physical health is compromised and emotional health is affected; this may result in spiritual blocks occurring. Reiki works to refocus and realign your energy to get your entire body working at its clearest and most optimal set point.

When you experience the journey of Reiki healing, it's really like a light switch going on inside of your mind, body, and soul; a sort of awakening occurs, and this awakening is different for everyone. Reiki seems to have an intelligence of its own, and healing goes to where it is needed. The healing may be directed to the chakras, your aura, your emotional body, your physical body, your spiritual body, or the centre points of disease within the body. It all depends on what is needed.

I experienced some incredible effects from Reiki healing and the attunement. I really want to make clear to everyone that Reiki DID NOT make me a medium or a psychic or give me any of the other abilities that I have, and it will not make you a medium or a psychic either. It may, however, clear your chakras and allow your intuitive abilities to develop further by clearing anything that may not be serving you at this time. There are seven main chakras as well a number of smaller ones within the human body. You are not just a physical body; you have a subtle body, too, of energy. The electrical magnetic field that surrounds you is your aura. The aura is made up of colours that look like the rainbow, and they shift and change to more dominant colours depending on what you are experiencing within your life. Your aura can hold the dominant colour of your spirit.

Your chakras transmit information from your aura, which represents the blueprint of your body. Your chakras hold information about your past pain and trauma; these are imprints into the auric field. These imprints affect your emotional, physical, and spiritual health.

What I have learned over the years is the importance the chakras play within the role of healing. This is a centre point that I always refer to when I conduct my soul healing and coaching sessions.

I can intuitively pick up spiritual or emotional blocks that are within your aura, as your chakra or body is talking to me, telling me what needs to be cleared. There are a number of books out there explaining the chakras and the aura, so if you are interested in learning, go to your public library or bookstore and pick one up or find a Reiki Master who is teaching Reiki.

So what did Reiki do for me? Well, I needed a lot of spiritual healing to help me move forward from past experiences. The experiences I had endured were keeping me from moving forward on my life path. I needed to believe in myself more, trust myself more, and know that I was worthy of receiving and giving others some very important healing and information. I really think Reiki saved my life and was a huge factor in healing my past.

After my Reiki courses, I once again got the urge to further my studies, so I started once again on my psychology degree. I was excited but also felt hindered by this quest, as it was taking me away from my spiritual path and being able to focus solely on my company.

I completed three more courses and decided to put everything on hold for the time being. I picked up a magazine and saw an ad reading, "Become a Certified Life Coach." Well the nudge came pretty fast from my intuition, and I heard the word *yes* to the left of my ear.

This was not an internal voice, and it was not my intuition; it was an outward voice, and no physical person was there. My clairaudience was back once more, even though it felt like it had left for a while. Perhaps it was best that it had!

So I listened to the voice and enrolled in the course. It would still take me a year to completely understand my purpose, as I kept getting nudges that not all was complete. Yes, I had a couple of moments of frustration and doubt. Was this really what I was supposed to do? Maybe I was crazy and should give up.

One morning I awoke to find my husband not beside me at 7:00 a.m. I went downstairs, and there he was, sitting on the couch, very much in pain. I rushed to him and asked what was happening. He said he had severe upper back pain. We rushed him to emergency, and he was taken away. I took my son to school and dropped my little one off at my mother-in-law's. I hurried back to the hospital, and my husband was all set up in a room, hooked up to machines. I spoke with the doctor and nurse about what was happening. Angels, they were; they saw my fear, no doubt. My husband, being the calm man he is, kept a positive attitude. "I don't think I had a heart attack." Of course, I wasn't about to agree until I had all the results back. I stayed with him as long as I could, and then I left to go pick up my son. When I left the hospital and sat in my car, I cried and prayed. I wasn't angry, just very, very afraid. After all, my husband was my best friend; he is one of my life guides this time around and the father of our children.

That evening I did long distance Reiki and saw him the next morning. He said he had started feeling better in the evening, so I asked him what time that was. It was around the same time I had done my distance healing. I would do another healing the next day, but on the third day I didn't do this practice. When I came in on the morning of the fourth day, he said he didn't do well that third evening and that the doctors were still running some tests. "They said I didn't have a heart attack but are now thinking maybe I did." We were all a little confused, and I felt a little guilty not doing the Reiki. I told him the story, and he laughed (what a good sport), so I began doing it again, and each night I did it he felt better. The diagnosis was pericarditis from an unknown origin. He had developed it. He remained in the hospital for almost ten days. As soon as he got home, I got busy with Reiki. It was an experience that I speak about in each one of my Reiki courses because it was so powerful.

I did Reiki on my husband three days in a row, for about two hours each time. He immediately fell asleep, and I worked extensively on his heart chakra. The energy surrounding his heart chakra was thick and mud-like, and I was becoming very tired during my healings, thinking that I could no longer do them. It would take me months before I could actually do a healing on him again. The doctors were amazed at how well he recovered and asked what he was doing. "My wife is doing Reiki on me!" he said.

The doctor nodded and smiled. "I have heard of that." Once again, proof was being provided to me on the power of universal energy.

As I was continuing with my company, sales were coming in but not enough to keep us financially afloat. So I took a part-time job in the evenings and on weekends when I didn't have clients. This gave me room during the day to take care of my two boys. My smallest one was still in pre-school, and my oldest was in grade two. I would have many more years ahead of me until I would feel financially safe. Daycare cost $1,300 a month, and I really wasn't happy about putting my children into a daycare. I did try once or twice, but something would always happen that would make me see that this wasn't in anyone's best interest. I got a job at the local hospital with great pay, and within one week the pipes at the daycare burst. I had to drive my kids to my father-in-law's place for a week, which was about 45 minutes each way. After everything was fixed at the daycare, I ended up getting extreme headaches, where I had trouble concentrating. Then the kids and I got the flu all at the same time, so I wasn't able to take them to the daycare. Then our van broke down! Hmm, was the universe trying to tell me something? As my husband and I were sitting in the car one afternoon after picking up our sons, we both knew. Full-time work for me was not part of the plan, not yet. It was interesting, though. My client load increased when I had more time. As soon as my son went into pre-school, I was provided with more clients. When my husband had a weekend off, the weekend would be full of clients. When both of my kids were in school, I was full with clients. It was amazing; all comes to you when you are ready to receive!

So I would work part-time while I put together my coaching programs, and at times I really felt like Archangel Michael and my guides were guiding me doing this. Many evenings and days I would wait, until I got the information, and then I would begin to write and put my programs together. I would spend countless hours making sure everything was perfect, and as soon as I was finished, life seemed to take another turn.

In one of my moments, lying in the bathtub, I heard the word *writing. Writing,* I thought. Well, I was already writing a book (not this one, another one that was entirely different, which would one day disappear from my computer completely), so I started the journey of writing newsletters.

One day while I was taking a walk, I heard the word *channeling,* and I started to get all sorts of information coming through from the world of Spirit; it was obvious I was going through another shift with this world. The spirit world was trying really hard to get my attention and to show me what I was capable of.

SPIRITUAL LIFE COACHING WITH THE AFTERLIFE

Becoming a life coach made so much sense to me. Coaching allowed me to utilize all of my previous education and experiences. I had already done so much healing on my own, and my life was moving swiftly in the right direction. I wanted to do more for others than just readings and healings. I knew my capability to help others was endless, and I would be shown I was correct later on in my journey.

I thought offering my readings was enough; I mean, it's so healing to hear from a loved one on the other side, and I knew readings were always going to be my first and foremost responsibility. However, I intuitively knew I needed to offer more services, and life coaching was one of them and the right direction for me.

So I looked at the different options I could offer and put a program together for my clients. It didn't make sense to me to offer coaching sessions unless I was also offering a reading with them. Spirit always gives me so much information, and when I tune into my own abilities, the soul usually speaks or screams at me and tells me what it needs, so I felt it was important to offer a combination session to my clients that would be able to utilize all of me! All of my gifts, abilities, and knowledge.

The ego is very intelligent and in most cases is really comfortable where it sits, meaning it doesn't always want to heal. Healing is hard work, but it can be fun and very rewarding too! So I needed to design a specific program that would help a person in all areas of his or her life — a program a person would commit to.

Putting a coaching program together isn't the easiest thing to do, at least not for me, and I still had that little voice inside my head that spoke of fear. My "ego" kept telling me people wouldn't take me seriously; after all, I talked to dead people, and my degree wasn't finished yet! Deep within my soul, I knew I could help people, and I knew my programs would change people's lives for the better, forever! My guides and angels were giving me positive information that my intuition was strong, so I knew I was ready for the next level.

I had put all my fears aside and surrendered to God. Because if this was something I was to do, then my guides and angels would help me. And guess what? They did! *And so would the dead!*

Before I could develop the perfect program, I was met with all sorts of obstacles. These obstacles were placed appropriately for me to learn from. My guides and angels were right on top of everything, making sure I was continuously learning and experiencing for my soul's growth.

Throughout the entire process, I continually brought myself back into meditation so I could clearly speak with my higher self and my spirit guides to ensure I understood all the information they were providing me with.

I was told time and time again in my meditations and in my dreams that the tools I was to use were to be used for only specific purposes and that each person I was to help would come to me with a different story and a very different healing, one from the next; however, there was a catch! Each and every person I would ever coach would have or would currently be going through something I had already gone through myself before, which I had already healed from. I was also told that if I was coaching clients with grief over a lost loved one, their loved ones would help me with my coaching sessions. Was the spirit world going to send me clients?

If I told you how some of my clients have found me, you would be a believer in the spirit world's sending me clients! For instance, I had a client who was looking for something completely different from my services, but my website kept coming up for him, for no obvious reason. Another client kept seeing my website everywhere; she had heard my name and met other people who were named Marnie in unusual places. Each and every time this happened, she kept thinking of my website and had an urgency to email me. I also had a client tell me she woke up one night and saw a beam of light by her bed, and her angel told her she needed to take all of her Reiki training with me!

Some days I am amazed! I hear my clients' stories, and many times it's like seeing myself in the mirror from years before! The benefit and understanding I can bring to my clients is undeniable. And to think I was scared that one day I couldn't help people!

The information that was being provided to me for my coaching program was so customized to the soul and to the individuals I helped that I ended up naming the program Soul Enhancement™ and legally trademarked this name. It was another step on my journey.

What is so unique about this program is that I work within the energy of the soul and the energy from the Afterlife. Remember in the beginning of this book where I explained a little information about the soul? Well, we really do carry all of our knowledge about our past and present, our soul lessons, and our soul contract with us. I was taught by my guides how to identify the blocks and this contract so I would know exactly how to help another soul — another person — with his or her life journey. This type of coaching takes a lot of concentration and the utilization of all my gifts and abilities. Many times during the development of my program, I would awaken around 3:00 a.m. and have an urge to get writing on my coaching program. This happens frequently. Spirit doesn't always worry about what time it is in our world! I was never a morning person; Spirit has been training me well to be one, though.

It was then when the spirit world came forward to provide me with all sorts of images and information. It felt like my head was being uploaded with a ton of information. When all is quiet and you are able to focus, this is when Spirit can talk to you without interruptions or fear from your conscious mind or the ego.

During this time, I was told deceased loved ones would come through before and during the coaching program, if needed, to provide me with some imperative information to help my clients. This process would not only help the clients; it would also help the soul on the other side find closure.

I was a little shocked at first. I mean, I knew the dead could provide so much detail and information, but they also wanted to help out with the coaching? Well how cool is that? The dead really do want to help us heal!

When I am in a reading, speaking with a loved one, the other side uses a specific healing symbol that tells me they need to heal with the loved ones who have survived them. This symbol tells me that things have happened in the past, and now emotions and situations need to be healed. Once the client and I are ready to step into the healing/reading, the rest of the information will follow.

My final program (The Soul Enhancement™ program) would then be designed in order to help my client and the world of spirit heal if needed!

If healing is needed with the Afterlife, sometimes the spirit world shows up before the hour my client is to arrive and may specifically provide me with details about the client and the deceased, leaving me a better understanding of what kind of healing I may perhaps enter into with my client. It doesn't always happen, though many times it does. *Spirit is always around when needed, and not every spirit needs to heal!*

One evening I was on my way to a group reading, and halfway there a male spirit showed up in the back seat of my car! I only could see an outline of him, but I sensed it was a father figure. I then asked why he was here. He said he had passed away and was the father of one of the ladies in the group reading. I felt he belonged to the lady who organized the group reading, but I wasn't able to hear him properly. After all, my concentration was on driving and finding the place. But I knew he was with me all the way! Well, he was so eager to speak! I almost had to start delivering messages immediately so he wouldn't hang around so much! He ended up indeed being the father of the lady who had organized the group reading, and he stayed around all the way through the session and thanked me in the end. There is never a dull moment in my life!

After taking a close look at how much Spirit wanted to help me with my coaching program, I needed to make sure I could offer my clients a wide variety of services. I was provided with options, though; after all, it was my company, and Spirit was well aware of this. So if another person had an interest in the coaching program but was unsure if this was for him or her, that person could start out with a combination session, a reading, or a spiritual assessment. *Sometimes it's so divinely organized!*

However, I found over the years that some people were holding judgment about their parents or loved ones coming through and offering substantial advice on how to move forward within their lives. The "ego" got in the way — oh, that darn ego!

As a Spiritual Life Coach, I have a variety of tools and knowledge I can incorporate into my sessions. Not only do I need to be able to jump from my left brain to my right brain quickly and to be able to listen to my clients one hundred percent, but I need to have an open mind and heart. The many spirits in the spirit world can get a little chatty if you let them. They mean well, though, so their help is only used as a secondary resource for the coaching programs.

One of the things I noticed within each one of my clients was the profound change that they were experiencing while going through my Soul Enhancement™ Life Coaching Program. The reason each one of my clients was getting such good results was that they were also learning how to identify and release the "ego," or "shadow self," and embrace their own light.

The "ego" is a false identity; it is not the true self. It is characterized by negative judgment of the self and will control the quality of your life. It will control your self-confidence, which can produce negative self-esteem. The ego is associated with fear; the fear reinforces the ego.

Each week we would work on a specific level and chakra, which allowed a unique healing process to take place within all of my clients. Remember, for me it's all about the timing and steps, as no individual is ever the same. I have been able to time exactly when someone is about to enter a huge awakening or healing, and this happens like clockwork each and every time with my clients. The ego begins to stir, and my guides and angels are always ready to give me a heads up so I can help my client through the transition. To my continual amazement, the guidance I receive from my spirit guides and the spirit world is 100% correct. Let's say I never judge or disregard the information that comes from the other side.

Years ago when my clients were going through my coaching process, I began to notice a unique change within myself, too. Even though I had released all of my old fears, a new healing would surface, which I would work diligently on to clear.

This was the time when I began to suffer extreme stomach pains, and I was being challenged repeatedly in all sorts of areas of my life. I knew my pain was much more than a solar plexus issue.

I would end up in the hospital twice with extreme stomach pain and no diagnoses. So I took control of my health. I had already weeded out processed foods, some meats, and dairy. Based on the bloating and cramping, it sounded like I had perhaps developed gluten intolerance. I went off of gluten (wheat) for two weeks and felt great. I went back to eating wheat, and the pain and bloating began, so of course I took myself off products with gluten and began losing weight and feeling good.

I highly suggest that if you do think you may have gluten intolerance, have your doctor provide the right tests before you begin to self-diagnose as I did. I had been off gluten for so long before I decided to get blood work done, and it came back negative, meaning I wasn't gluten intolerant. And under no circumstances was I going to start eating wheat again so I could get a proper diagnosis! I knew it worked for me, so I was satisfied with that.

As we let go of certain emotions and habits that are based on the ego, we begin to release what I call *energy toxins*. As we heal our energy bodies, our physical bodies begin to shift also. This shift may cause a reaction to take place within the physical body needing to release waste. This waste can be energy, emotion, or even bodily fluids. It's whatever your body may need at the time to begin the increase in raising its vibration. It's a well-known fact that soul healing or awakening symptoms do exist when one begins to embrace the journey of awareness and spiritual awakening. These symptoms are generally normal. However, I always tell my clients to never assume anything and to please seek medical attention if any of their symptoms increase, are very uncomfortable, or change in frequency.

You are in control of the process; ask your angels and guides to help you, and if it becomes uncomfortable, ask them to give you a break for a while. God, your angels, or your guides would never inhibit you or put you though unnecessary pain (unless it was part of your spiritual contract).

Some possible signs that your soul is healing and your vibrational frequency is reaching a higher and more positive level include★:

1. **Body aches around the neck, shoulder, back, and stomach.** Once the energy surrounding the astral body begins to shift, the muscular systems seem to shift, too. The negative energy is beginning to be released; it needs to awaken first before it can heal.
2. **Crying.** Crying is good. It means you are releasing old thoughts and emotions. You may start crying for no apparent reason, and that's okay. It is a good time to get a journal out and start to write your experiences. The body will talk to you; it will tell you what it needs, because it's a messenger for the soul.
3. **Anger within yourself.** Once you become aware of your actions and others' previous actions, you may feel regret, remorse, and anger at yourself or at the people who hurt you. This does pass — when you start the journey of forgiveness. Please make sure you always have someone to talk to when you are going

through healing. Seek guidance from spiritual professionals when needed; it helps to have another person's opinion to put your thoughts into perspective. This isn't a good time to rely on family or friends to speak with. You may withdraw from family members and friends for the time being. This transition shall pass, too. It's important to remember to forgive yourself on this journey. This is a great time for self-care. Self-care can be anything from massage, yoga, or meditation to working out at the gym, taking a walk, reading a book, buying a new outfit, getting a pedicure or a manicure, or simply enjoying some soft music for a while.

4. **Feelings of loneliness and not belonging.** These will last only a short time, no more than a month. It's important to take time to see the world around you, take time to adjust to your new lenses! Read, read, and read. Get some good self-help books.
5. **Weight changes, usually loss.** As you become more aware and withdraw from a trance-like state, you also become more aware that your body is a divine vessel carrying a very important mission! It is carrying your soul's journey. So be careful what you put in it!
6. **Career changes, relationship changes.** And finally you begin the path of awakening (seeing your life more clearly).
7. **Allergic reactions to lower vibrational foods.** You may start to experience stomach upset when eating processed foods or foods that have been genetically modified. Eat high vibrational foods as much as you can. This includes organic fruits and vegetables, non-genetically modified foods, and foods that are living — not coming from a package.

* Please note: Not everyone has the same experiences with soul healing or in my coaching programs. You will go through whatever it is you need to heal.

It's important to note that not all steps are the same for everyone, and no souls are the same just as no fingerprints are the same. Knowing you and your soul and understanding yourself are what's important in healing or awakening.

One of the difficult attributes of soul healing is learning how to let go of what no longer serves you. For instance, you may no longer resonate with people who surround you. When you take a close look at them, you see that they were no good for you anyway, and your soul may have been trying to tell you that for years.

You begin to see the world with a whole new set of eyes — eyes that are wide open and healthy. You are learning to take the blinders off. These eyes now become connected to a healthier mind and a healthier soul. You will see what doesn't serve you, and you will learn to maneuver through it, change it, and move into alignment with your true self and higher purpose. You may even start getting sudden inspiration to do positive things, such as moving, walking, writing, or taking up a spiritual development class. It's your soul communicating with you, so listen!

Embrace the journey! It's important to remember, though, that due to free will, our guides cannot intervene or help us with our journey unless we ask them to. And they can only go so far; they will not step into your path of growth and will not provide information or guidance that would have a negative impact on you, and your personal growth falls into the category. Most importantly, be aware of your intention at all times. If you ask your guides to help you and it's not part of your highest intention, forget it! You will only receive what you need.

I do want to mention that healing can occur even without the help of your angels and guides. Each soul is very powerful and has been through many lifetimes, which means it carries a variety of knowledge with it. Healing is about tapping into the unconscious mind and learning how to heal the past. Everything you have ever experienced, you have done because your soul has requested it of you. Remember, everyone is your teacher, teaching you what needs to be, and you will be tested time and time again to ensure you have learned the lesson or haven't forgotten it. When I see a lesson coming forward, I always say God is testing me again! I passed the first time, so I will pass this one too! I just need to bring out my healing tools to overcome the lesson.

Some individuals can't seem to step into a healing realm and realize the lesson that is right in front of them. Their egos are stopping them from seeing the truth, which can be scary at times. I have learned over the years that people must go through their own healing to be strong advocates and guides to help others through their healing.

Entering into a profession where there is a constant surrounding of pain can lead one to feel emotionally, spiritually, and physically drained and disconnected. This may result in one experiencing burnout or depression. I make a constant effort to ensure that I remain plugged in to life, which can be hard to do sometimes. Making a strong connection and remembering that everything I have ever experienced has brought me to where I am today helps me stay proactive within my life and not reactive to the situations at hand.

If a person is busy disconnecting from the real world and remaining a victim, how on earth is one going to hear the messages from one's soul, not to mention hear the messages from the Afterlife and one's angels? You need to be aware and connected to the moment so you can hear the messages your soul, the universe, and your loved ones are trying to tell you.

Messages from your soul are meant to help you on your journey. Remember, healing starts from within, and learning how to forgive your past — such as by looking for the gratitude within a situation, understanding the lesson, and moving forward — is a way you can start the healing. I have provided you with a small healing affirmation that you can say daily to help you with forgiveness. Please note: There is much more to forgiving than this, but it will steer you in the right direction.

Forgiveness is the first and vital step in any spiritual healing or practice. We must learn to love all with our hearts. This doesn't mean that we accept what the other has done, but we acknowledge the hurt, acknowledge that your "ego" is only trying to protect you, and the pain is your soul talking. Again, you don't need to forget the person; you do need to learn how to forgive the person and the circumstance. Learn to understand why it happened, which will result in you letting go of the person without carrying feelings of anger, resulting in you forgiving the person and the situation in your own way; a healthy way! Remember, you experienced it because your soul needed you to.

Affirmations are here to help fill your head with positive thoughts, which will allow the mind to experience positive emotions; the body will follow and react to the emotions. Even if you don't believe it yet, say it daily for about six weeks and watch how your mind, body, and soul will believe it to be true! Before you do this affirmation, close your eyes take a couple of relaxing deep breaths and quickly meditate first to center your mind with your soul.

Affirmation:

I am acknowledging my fear and my anger, so I can heal. I understand that my "self" is only trying to protect me, and that is why I feel pain and hurt within my heart and soul. I am a healthy, wonderful, and forgiving person. I know that I am the co-creator of my life and I have chosen to live my life with happiness and love. I am moving forward on my life path as a powerful, loving human being. I ask Archangel Michael to release any negative thoughts or energies from my mind, body, and soul regarding _____ (put person, place, or situation in the blank line) and send these energies back to where they came from with love. I ask God to place me within His loving light so I can heal and grow from my experience with_____ (put person, place or situation in the blank line). Amen.

INTUITION

So let's talk again about intuition! I get asked a lot about intuition, and it can be very confusing, to say the least. The word intuition comes the Latin word *intueri,* which when translated means "to look inside or to contemplate." Even though intuition is a common word in the new-age spiritual movement, it's been around a long time. It has been a subject in psychology and part of the supernatural studies. No matter where it came from, we all have it. Some of us are born with an active right brain, which may make us more intuitive. When used properly — that is, by listening and following through — your intuition increases. Intuition cannot be taught in a weekend or even a week-long course, but you can receive some valuable tools to help you recognize and increase your intuition.

A psychic or medium is intuitive, but being intuitive is very different from being a psychic or medium. The simplest way I can explain it is that intuition comes from within. However, mediums are also psychic, meaning they get their information from a universal source of energy and loved ones; they call themselves psychic mediums or mediums. All mediums are psychic, but not all psychics are mediums. Mediums can tap into the spiritual realm and receive information from other sources including loved ones. A psychic is someone who receives information from a universal source of energy, including the client's energy, not from loved ones on the other side. The majority of "psychic mediums" or "mediums" have been born with these abilities and have had some sense of connection with the other side since childhood. As I have said before, you can't have one without the other if you call yourself a medium or psychic medium. For me, the connection with the Afterlife is very strong, which is why I offer two different types of readings. You have the option to book a Medium Reading or a Spiritual Psychic Reading, and I have chosen to call myself a spiritual medium.

Psychic abilities come from reading the energy around another person or subject. Mediumship is reading the energy from the other side — the souls in the Afterlife.

So how do you become intuitive? By increasing your self-esteem, believing in yourself, letting go of what no longer serves you in this life, embracing your life, forgiving your past by opening up your energy systems and your chakras, and acknowledging the intuitive hits (that little voice inside you) and following through with them. You increase your intuition by using your intuition.

How many times have you felt something and ignored the message, only to find out later you had been right? Your intuition is here to serve you through thoughts, which are energy; in fact, everything is energy in the world.

As humans, we have the ability to manifest great things in our lives by putting a positive thought to what it is we want to manifest in our lives. When you have a positive thought, you create a positive action, and up the spiral it goes. If you deny your own feelings and thoughts and your own warning system, you are denying the natural law of life and the law of attraction. Your own intuitiveness is unique to you. Once you have a good sense of it and how it works and use it diligently, it is then that you can use it to help others.

I have heard many times, and experienced myself, those moments when of uneasiness, such as when you first meet someone or are required to make a decision. Each and every time you think about the decision you need to make, you notice how something doesn't feel right. You have a sense of hesitation, a knot in your stomach, and you don't feel right with the issue at hand. Yet everyone else may be telling you the guy you just met is a great guy, so what you may be experiencing is fear of a relationship. Sometimes you get a job offer and everyone else thinks you're crazy not to take it, but that little voice is saying, "NO, DON'T DO IT."

Times like this can be confusing. Some people may not trust their inner voices, so instead, they seek others to provide the correct answers in the hopes that their inner doubt will disappear, and they feel relieved that if it doesn't work out, they can blame the other person, not themselves.

Another example is that maybe the person who has asked you out on a date is a great person, but maybe that person isn't great for you. Maybe someone else has been written on your path, and in order to meet that one, you must follow through with what your own heart or own intuition is telling you. It is your journey, after all. When you're dealing with intuition, it's really important to get out of your head and get into your heart. Listen to what your own energy is telling you.

When you listen to yourself — your intuitive guidance — your life becomes a lot easier, a lot more functional. Your intuition grows if you use it. If you don't, it's like a plant: It begins to die when not watered. You need to be persistent to understand and exercise your intuition.

For years I denied my psychic and medium abilities. I tried very hard to ignore the spirits I saw with my physical eyes and the information I received about others. I even ignored the intuitive information about myself! Why? Because I didn't trust myself. I had somehow been taught that the answers were with other people. Answers couldn't possibly be within me. I would think the answers to my life must somehow reside within a person who had more knowledge and education, was more mature, and on and on. It took me many years to get the nerve up to say, "I am going to listen!" First, I had to first understand that I was the one in charge of my life. My life belonged to me and God, and no one else.

Everyone needs to trust his or her own intuition! It can save your life or someone else's. Professional mediums or psychics need to trust the information they are receiving at all times. If you are not listening to your intuition and you are doing this form of work, how can you be relaying correct information? It takes a lot of trust and faith in yourself and in Spirit to deliver messages from the Afterlife.

I get a lot of questions from people, such as, "How do I know this is intuition and not just my 'ego' talking back to me?" I always tell my clients, and have to remind myself too, that the ego thinks it's your protector and tries to protect you from fearful situations. These situations are always a part of your personal and professional growth. Fear is normal when a person is faced with a life-threatening situation. Sometimes I refer to the ego as the *shadow self* for these reasons.

One way to identify if it's the ego or shadow self is to think of it this way: Let's say you meet someone and you get along really well; in fact, you like this person so much you start introducing them to your friends and family. Then you wake up one day and decide perhaps this person isn't for you — you start to think maybe you're rushing things, or perhaps you fear they will turn out just like all the others. This is your ego talking, not your intuition. If you are not seeing any red flags and the person hasn't done anything to change your perception of them, you can bet you are afraid to move forward and the ego is trying to rule, or let's say protect you in a way — just not in a good way.

You can't get rid of the ego, so it's important to identify it when needed. Your ego is also connected to your healing. If you haven't healed certain aspects of your life, your ego will remember and keep that pain alive — another reason to make sure you are healing your soul!

The ego is triggered by fear, and fear is FALSE EVIDENCE APPEARING REAL!

One of the easiest scenarios I can explain is this: When you have an idea and you get excited about it and start moving forward, you get the heart palpitating and the shivers going through your body, and you feel like you can take on the world. That's your intuition saying, "Let's get moving!" Then all of a sudden the "ego" steps in and says, "Hey! You don't have enough education to do that! No one is going to listen to you! Remember the last time you tried that and you failed? You're going to fail again!" Get my drift? This is the ego at play! It doesn't want you to get hurt again, so it tries to keep you safe and sound, tucked away in your own fears, not letting you grow and experience all that life truly has to offer.

It's important to note, though, that not everyone who is in your life is to stay in your life. Sometimes you meet people and everything is great in the beginning, and later it begins to turn sour. Does this mean your intuition was wrong? Absolutely NOT! Whatever you needed from that specific relationship is no longer required. Perhaps you outgrew the person, or it's simply time to move forward to the next level of your life.

This is where a lot of people get stuck. They dwell on trying to understand the *whys* and *how-comes* without focusing on the gratitude and the *what-next*. Regard what I said earlier: Everything and everyone is your teacher. Ask yourself, "What did I learn about myself and life from this experience?" Look for the positives; I know you can find them.

No one is exempt from painful or happy experiences within this life; your intuition is your link to your soul, so listen.

Once you have mastered your intuition (and, believe me, we are always learning and improving), you can start relaxing and realize that we are all very similar and have had similar experiences. No one is a victim unless a person decides this is where he or she wants to stay. However, there is and always will be a better way to live.

I also want to take this time to clarify why I feel it is so important to explain this. In the beginning of the book, I mentioned I was married before and had two abusive relationships. I have had many more relationships that were abusive, supported by my lack of self-esteem. I don't think I overcame the deaths of my mother and my father until I was well into my thirties, and when I began to start my own family. I went through a huge growth period, and the outcome was the development of self-esteem that allowed me once again to embrace those gifts I have had since birth.

Part of my own soul contract was learning how to do exactly this. Not everyone's contract within this world is the same. Mine is unique to me, as yours is unique to you. I had to learn how to embrace my abilities and learn how to help people, including myself.

I felt my contract also stated that I needed to trust in God and have trust in myself. I learned that I am a powerful person, and I understand that I carry the ability to guide and help change people's lives. It's one of the reasons I was born.

However, it took me many years to learn this lesson because my life was set up to play out the way I was spiritually intended to learn it. In my earlier years, I always seemed to take the harder road; that was only because I was conditioned to do so. Sometimes I thought if it wasn't hard, it wasn't meant to be. Oh, how I have grown up!

I know today that if I had had more self-esteem and had learned how to trust my intuition, I may have not found myself in some really difficult relationships and jobs. However, not all is lost, as with each difficult road I chose, I also became stronger and more knowledgeable, and my experiences gave me the strength to look deeper into my past, my lifestyle, and my reason for being alive.

You see, I hold no bitter emotions towards anyone or any situation I have lived in. How did I do that? Now comes the second part of developing your intuition: awakening your highest potential and learning how to forgive.

Anger with the past holds lots of power — the power of destroying the spirit and the physical body. Anger does not hold any solutions; it only holds negative power. Learning to let go of anger is one of the most profound experiences I have ever had, and I have had many. When you live your life from a complete state of love, life changes, and so does everyone else. How can that be? I learned to release any negative perceptions and embrace only the positive. I like to say I began the journey of mastering my own journey. I realize now that I was the one who got myself into these poor relations. I'm not saying I created the situations; somehow these situations mirrored me. I drew forward to me what I needed to experience in order to grow, and we draw to us the energy we send out.

Now if someone had told me that when I left an abusive relationship, I may have told that person where to go! So I am going explain exactly what I mean by putting it into simple terms. Along with having no self-esteem, I was suffering from abandonment issues. I wasn't listening to my internal guidance, let alone the guidance from Spirit. I wanted to find someone who I felt could complete me. I hadn't yet realized or learned that I was already complete and that no one was ever going to make me happy unless I learned how to make myself happier first.

Your intuition is your compass telling you what is right or wrong. If you do not have faith or believe in your own self or do not have a goal, you are simply disconnected from the self, from your soul.

When your intuition is strong, you can effectively start to become more aware of your surroundings, your feelings, and your emotions and then perhaps the feelings and emotions of others. Remember earlier when I mentioned how Reiki was an integral part of my healing? Reiki helped me release deep, destructive emotions, which were energy blocks within my energetic and physical body. These blocks were contributing to the physical illnesses that were holding me back from my true calling. By clearing the energy blocks, I began to listen to the spirit within me. Another effective way to develop your intuition is through meditation. As you begin to learn how to silence the mind with meditation, you also can start hearing the inner voice that is inside of you — inside all of us.

A guessing game is also a great way to exercise your intuition. Pick out some gemstones and put them under your pillow. Close your eyes and reach under the pillow, and guess which stone you have by keeping your hand closed and focusing on which stone is in your hand. You may be surprised how many times you are right; doing this will build the trust within you.

Intuition is like a muscle; the more you use it, the better it works, and yet it never leaves you if you haven't used it in a while. If you are getting intuitive hits all the time and ignore them, what message are you sending your soul? "I don't believe you, and I don't trust you."

This is why trust is so imperative with intuitive development. The better you trust yourself, the better your intuition becomes. This isn't only about feelings; thoughts are important, too. You would never have a thought about doing something positive if you didn't have the capability to make it work for you. I have to emphasize POSITIVE.

Anytime you have a thought that is tied to something negative, it's not necessarily your intuition talking; it could be the "ego" speaking.

This is because intuition is of the soul, and at no time does a healthy soul put you or another person at risk of being hurt on any level.

This now leads us to the understanding that the heart is also a doorway to the soul. If you are angry, bitter, living within the past, always trying to get even, or too busy hating yourself and the world, you are not going to trust the world, God, or even yourself. So trust and love are also imperative to your intuitive development!

How can being more intuitive help you? Intuition is a vital component to your soul. When you listen to it, you learn your life lessons faster, life is a little easier, and you make far fewer mistakes than when you are not using it. Intuitive people also make excellent nurses, therapists, counselors, teachers, lawyers, law enforcement officers, and parents — anyone who has a job helping or dealing with other people. Let's face it — the world needs more love and compassion in it!

Everyone can feel and sense the energy that is around another person; you don't even need to be intuitive. However, it takes a trained mind and soul to understand exactly what it is you are sensing around another person's energy or aura. Not everything is at is seems. Your own inner spirit must come from a place of healing and love, meaning you need to have done your own healing to truly understand impressions that you are receiving of another person. It's so easy to put judgment on someone if you yourself are living within a negative frame of mind.

So let's say you are sitting on a plane and a person sits down beside you. All of a sudden you get an uneasy feeling and want to move to another seat. You make the connection that your feeling of uneasiness must be coming directly from the person who just sat down beside you. You take a look at this person and feel and sense all sorts of things that provide you with negative thoughts and assumptions towards that person.

A person who is a little more spiritually aware or positively intuitive may see the person who sat beside you as a person in need of healing and hopefully take that opportunity to send loving thoughts, prayer, and energy to the individual to help him or her on the journey. Imagine what the world would be like if we all sent positive thoughts and energy to everyone on a daily basis! The vibration frequency of the planet would change considerably, for the better! This is one of my wishes for all of humanity.

However, the person who isn't so spiritually connected to their soul may take the images they are receiving and believe that this person beside them must be bad or has done something bad — why else would they feel this way? This thought has produced the right conditions to allow the ego to kick into high gear and awaken the call of judgment. I can tell you firsthand that the person you are secretly judging can feel your thoughts too! So don't expect any smiles or happy words coming your way. Your thoughts are powerful, so choose them wisely!

What's really happening is that everyone and everything that has ever lived walks around with this huge antenna on the top of his or her head. We are all walking antennas, functioning on all different psychic frequencies. Everything is energy — our thoughts, our feelings, our memories. The person who sat down beside you could have been having a bad day, or perhaps that person was just laid off from work and is thinking poorly of his or her boss or the company he or she worked with. A person never really knows, so should we place judgment quickly? Believe me, if you are in a bad situation, you will feel real fear that has no judgment to it; it's fear that gets your heart beating fast, and you make a judgment call immediately, with no hesitation — there is no second-guessing when you are dealing with real fear. The ego is about judgment.

Intuition is also contained in the right hemisphere of the brain and within the solar plexus, or upper stomach chakra. Not only do you need to exercise the right brain to increase intuition, you need to keep the power center of your chakra, the solar plexus, clean and clear by following the guidelines above and exercising forgiveness and love.

A LITTLE BIT ABOUT THE BRAIN:

LEFT HEMISPHERE	RIGHT HEMISPHERE
(Objective and rational)	(Emotions, intuition, & creativity)
Thinks in words	Thinks in pictures
Governs language, speech, reading, & writing	Coordinates signing
Analyzes issues by breaking them apart	Can see many things simultaneously

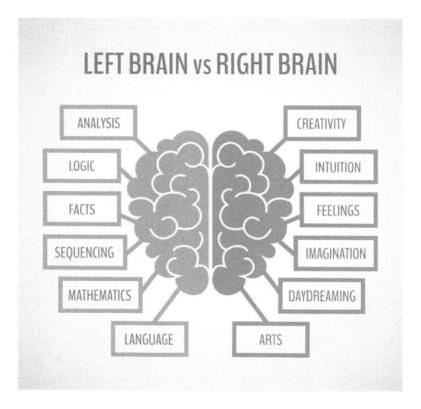

MEDITATION

Meditation is about silencing the mind and learning to focus. The best way to learn about meditation is to first learn about your breathing. For the purpose of this book, I'm only going to provide some simple techniques that I started out using. The best time to meditate is when you are alone, or at least in a quiet area. I don't recommend meditating in a car or at work where you're required to have complete attention.

To start off, get a nice white unscented candle (which also attracts Spirit) and light it. I want you to look at the flame, and as you do, take some nice deep breaths in and out, about two or three times. I want you to close your eyes and do a body check. See what may be causing you pain or stress and try to simply breathe into the area where you are feeling the stress, and release it. Send out loving energy and breath to the stress.

For protection purposes, please call on Archangel Michael and your spirit guides and ask that they protect you from any energies that don't serve you at this moment in time. Give them permission to remove the negative energies around you and around your home that may be causing you unneeded emotional of physical stress. When you have completed this, I want you to take another couple of deep breaths in and out, and make sure you are breathing deep from the core of your stomach and that you are relaxed.

Open your eyes and look at the flame. Visualize a beautiful rose in the middle of the flame; watch how each petal of the rose opens with each number you count. Count from 1 through 5; on the fifth number, see how all the petals are completely open and each has a number on it. Keep your eyes focused on the rose and notice how eventually the numbers simply seem to fade away. Allow the rose to completely disappear, leaving you to see only the flame in the candle. If you have a thought come through when you are doing this exercise, simply acknowledge the thought and breathe through the emotion. Remember, your goal is to exercise the mind to quiet itself so you can relax and learn how to focus on one thing at a time.

This is where it gets tricky, as most people end up stopping, becoming frustrated in thinking they can't keep theirs mind clear or focused. We have more than 70,000 thoughts per day, so don't expect your meditation to be easy your first time around. You have to learn how to control your thoughts. So when I say acknowledge the thought, accept it, and then breathe through it, just carry on; it is absolutely normal. You are not a Buddhist monk who has been practicing meditation for years, but you know meditation does have many health benefits. It's about putting positive attention on your body and your soul with your positive thoughts.

You can keep going if you like. Once the rose has disappeared, you can set the intention that you would like to see more information about your life or your healing. By allowing the rose to disappear, you open up the flame to notice other images that the universe or your higher self would like to provide you with. All messages are for your highest good. This may also include a word or a symbol; it will be something you can relate to or understand.

After you have been practicing meditation for a while, perhaps you will be ready to tap into your higher self or receive guidance from your angels or spirit guides.

Before you start your meditation, you will need to set the intention of what it is you're doing. Are you meditating for relaxation purposes? Or are you in need of guidance?

If you are looking for guidance, have a pad of paper and a pen ready for the messages you may see within the flame, or you simply may start seeing them within your inner vision — and that's okay, too! Never put too much expectation on anything. Allow the information to flow. That way, you are not allowing the left brain or your ego to get in your way. Once you get the hang of getting the mind, body, and spirit connection moving, you will find everything gets a little easier.

POSTURE

You may be in a sitting position in a chair, sitting cross-legged, or lying down on your back (keep your legs apart and palms facing up). If you feel ungrounded at the time, then just keep your palms facing down.

BREATHING

Begin with an expansive breath. Breathe into the stomach, and expand into the chest, into the collarbone; breathe out slowly. Your stomach should be like a balloon inflating and deflating. Repeat the breath by slowly exhaling. Once you are relaxed, continue with your normal breathing; you don't want to hyperventilate during this time!

FINISHING OFF THE MEDITATION

There are ways to finish the meditation. You may focus on OHM (which is the most powerful mantra and corresponds to the Egyptian AMEN). You always need to give thanks to everything, especially when you are dealing with the higher realms of light.

You should meditate at least 5–10 minutes a day and try to increase your experience. It's also a good idea to keep a meditation journal so you can write down your experiences and any information that may be brought forward to you. Remember, this is an integral part of healing, as everyone receives messages from the spirit world on one level or another.

I also suggest taking some time after your meditation to concentrate and focus on developing your third eye. Meditation does do this; however, you can further develop your third eye by doing some focusing techniques. I suggest looking at the candle or a picture on the wall and keeping the focus on the item, allowing your visualization to focus so much that everything around the object begins to disappear. Please note that if you start to get a headache, you may be doing too much, so slow down and try again. Happy practicing!

SELF-ESTEEM AND THE SOUL

Self-esteem is something that each one of us is inherently born with, but it's years of experiences or lessons that can either enhance or lower our self-esteem. For example, if we are each a child of God and he only builds perfection, isn't each one of us perfect right from the beginning? Everyone is born special and unique in his or her own way. "Everything has beauty, but not everyone sees it." —Confucius

Growing up in a home where I knew I was loved but was a naturally shy person, it felt like the outside world was making me feel inadequate. I felt like something was wrong with me for being quiet — or was that just me mirroring back what I believed inside?

Remember back to the earlier part of this book, when I said my mother wasn't well? Well, she wasn't, but that didn't mean I was unwell, and that certainly did not mean I would become unwell. Our belief systems and value systems are based on what we have been taught — and taught to be truth. These teachings may come from people who love us, family member, teachers, caregivers, television, and/or the books we read. When we are children, we are clean slates, except for the past lives that begin to surface later on in life.

Remember, everyone is your teacher, teaching you something about life or his or her own value and belief system. It's important to have your own system in place; however, at times it can be more destructive than productive information.

When I look back at my earlier life, I was not only shy; I was also an introvert for many, many years. I don't think I began to really open myself up to my friends and family until my late twenties, and here I am today, 48 and opening up to the world about my life and my healing!

I found that once everyone got out of my way and let me be me without always asking me to be not so quiet or shy — and did not try to mold me into their own perfect vision of what they wanted — it was then that my self-esteem increased. Once my self-esteem increased, I became more of an extrovert. Yes, once an introvert, *not* always an introvert. Everyone can change if they want to; it's an option within the soul.

All I needed is what everyone else needs in life: a chance for self-expression without scrutiny or judgment! When you're always trying to fit into everyone else's molds and expectations, life can become really confusing and a little depressing, because you are never going to find the perfect fit, not from another's point of view. Your perfect fit comes from inside you, and it's important you find it for achieving complete happiness. When your soul feels complete, you will know it! Your spirit becomes unstoppable! And your self-esteem? It's at an all-time high, and that's good, because you need to love yourself first, before you can love anyone else!

I see a lot of me in my children today. Both of my children are very intuitive. I have one child who is an introvert at school, but when you get him home, he doesn't stop talking and he loves to try new things. I always laugh because one day I bet he will feel perfectly comfortable standing in front of a crowd talking. I can say this today as I try to focus my attention on all his qualities and capabilities, not his quietness or the things I think he needs to work on. If he feels he needs to work on something, I will be the first person to help him, but you won't find me pointing out many flaws within my children. They are who they are, and I love them unconditionally. They are my angels!

Sometimes as parents, teachers, or caregivers, we struggle to learn how to communicate with a child who may appear to have self-esteem issues or is just downright quiet. Sometimes our knowledge comes from our own expectations and perceptions. When my son was in preschool, I was confronted by a teacher who worked within the school system and who also new my oldest child. When I came in to pick up my youngest son, she looked at me and said, "I should have known this was your child. I think you really should get your children out more so they can learn to speak out and communicate better with other kids!" I looked at her and bit my tongue to what I might have said and instead told a truthful story.

I thanked her for her concern and said, "You know, you said that with my first son! However, this summer we went back to B.C., and on July 1st, Canada Day, we went down to a festival, and they had the local radio station there. The radio host was on the main stage and asked if there were any children in the crowd who would like to come up and speak about what Canada Day means to them. Well, my son, to my surprise, put his hand up, walked straight up to the stage, took the microphone, and began talking to about two or three hundred people on what Canada Day meant to him! The radio show host actually had to ask for the microphone back and joked that my son could take over the show if he wanted. Everyone laughed with excitement, and everyone clapped. My son stood proud and came back to his seat! Both my husband and I looked at him and gave him a big hug and said we were so proud of him, and I never asked why he did what he did. That was the day when I realized that each child and person who lives may be different but will always do what is right, when it is right, for their soul. For no soul is the same. For no person can be the same."

After I finished my story, her eyes went big, and I said, "Yes, my children are quiet, but they are smart, and they are good kids. We give them ample opportunities to meet people and to experience sports and anything else they need or want to experience that is healthy. Everyone develops differently in his or her own time." Perhaps the teacher needed to be reminded of this.

As parents, we have to remember that each child has been born in a person's family for a specific reason, and they chose you to be their parent, and you chose them to be your child. They need to not only to learn from you but to be unconditionally accepted by you, too. It's a universal law of family love, so just love them with all your heart and soul!

Not everyone is going to fit into our ideal boxes, and we need to become more aware of that now than ever before. Each and every person is to fulfill his or her life calling, and acceptance and love for all are the only things that are going to make this world a better place to live. I think we can see how the past has already taught us what works and what doesn't work.

I remember my teachers asking my parents why I was so shy. My father would just smile. "Yes, she is quiet." He knew that was me for now, but everyone else seemed to want to make a big deal about it, and I think I'm not alone in having experienced this. I was an introvert when I was young, but after my healing took place, I became an extrovert. Personally, I think we have a bit of both in all of us, all the time. There is absolutely nothing wrong with being an introvert or an extrovert. Both are normal, and I believe we can change based on the situations at hand. There is more to us than we know. But introverts seem to get admonished for it, like it's not normal. What is normal, anyway? I think normal is being happy and loving to all. Anything else is abnormal! We really live in an abnormal world, don't we?

Years ago when I was working through my psychology degree, I did a report on the connection between bulimia and the media, and, yes, I think there is a strong correlation there. As we grow up, we are being taught how we should look, feel, and act. These are process teachings that are all based on other people's perceptions, which include the media. And we are taught that we have a lot to gain by adopting some of those common perceptions, such as the concept that thin is sexier. Or that if you want to get ahead in life, you must be pretty or handsome! Is this really true? I don't think so! This process teaches people — mostly the younger generation — not to listen from their souls and to be led by others rather than leading themselves. Instead, we need to teach people that their personalities should unfold as they do. Not everyone is the same, and it's okay to be an individual; we are all so unique and special in our own way. You can inform your children of the importance of being healthy, doing what they love to do, being a good person, and the value of being in service to others and to the world. It's not productive to fill the heads of our children and other people with fear that will take them away from the most important element of living: happiness.

This can be hard, too — living inside this frame of thought with all the chaos that is happening in our world today. However, it's imperative that a person keeps focused on esteem issues and positive emotions. Remember, your thoughts create your reality, and your reality sets the stage for your energy field; if your energy field is unbalanced, the rest of your body, and maybe your life, will be too.

A healthy self-esteem and a good set of strong morals can work well for you in life.

When I was young, I never accepted what I was seeing or hearing from the other side, and this created a belief system in me that dampened my self-esteem. I knew I was experiencing voices and visualizations that others did not. I knew I had a keen sense of smell and had correct feelings and knowledge about other people. Some would say I was "street smart." My friends always felt comfortable confiding in me, and they still do today. You see, I started off as a sensitive child, so when I learned to embrace this "gift" (and I say *gift* literally, as not all people are capable of talking to the dead!), I learned to accept this ability. I surrendered to the possibility of its not being a defect or a curse, and I learned how to take control of it and make it manifest into something wonderful for me! I'm not trying to be boastful here, but the reality is that many children, and those who are highly sensitive to spirit energy, don't know what to do with their gifts or how to make these gifts work for them. This leaves them frustrated and perhaps even depressed. When this happens, a turn for the worse can often take place. Some people turn to alternative substances to numb the sensitivity; others turn inward and shut the world out.

Today I am a firm believer that if there were more information about the world of Spirit, being intuitive, and living a sensitive life and less judgmental reaction from people regarding this ability, perhaps life would be a little easier for some. Just because you can talk to dead people or you see a ghost doesn't always mean something is wrong. It means you have an exceptional mind that is capable of many things, with abilities that you should be happy with.

If you're up to it, I would like you to try this very simple exercise. Look at yourself in the mirror daily and say some positive words to yourself every morning. This can simply be a mantra. You can also write the words on your mirror with a washable marker so you can look at them when you brush your teeth or are combing your hair. A really easy mantra is *I am a happy, confident, and loving person.*

When working on your self-esteem, it's important to learn how to place God's white light protection around you. You can simply ask God and your angels to place a cocoon of white light around you for protection and healing while you are going through your own healing and/or when you know you are going to be around some negative or heavy energy. Putting yourself in God's white light will only protect you; you will still learn any lessons you need to learn — it's not going to stop that. Self-esteem is a learned behavior that, once harnessed, will open many doors for your personal and professional life, and your intuition goes hand-in-hand with the process.

You're more in control of your life than you think you are — believe me. God doesn't create monsters; we do. We do this with our thoughts, our beliefs, and our value systems.

I'm sure you are aware by now that I speak what I feel, and my words are meant for you to think about and believe in whatever you want. I am the messenger, and I hope you are hearing me loud and clear so far. But you are the one who has the choice of how you want to live. You don't have to live with an old story; all stories can be changed. Yours, too!

I have provided you with an affirmation and another mantra! Say it daily and change the wording to fit your situation. For the mantra, you can put it on your phone or anywhere you look frequently!

Every cell in my body vibrates with energy and health. I am a confident [woman or man] who attracts healthy relationships and business ventures. I believe in myself, and so do others. I have close family and friends who value and see the beauty within me. I am a loving soul, and I trust the process of life and myself. I nourish my mind, body, and spirit daily and see the light and beauty that is continuously within me.

Mantra: I am healthy, confident, and full of loving energy!

ACCEPTING MY SOUL'S CALLING

Everything I had gone through in my past was in place to help me remember and see why I was here. As I began accepting my abilities once again, I began to channel more. I had done this previously when I was a young teenager. Actually, I do have the abilities to be a physical medium. This is where I let the spirit enter my energy body and the spirit begins to speak through me. I have had to learn over the years not to enter into the practice, so now I let Spirit come only so close to me. I can already hear and feel Spirit, but it can be very draining, not to mention dangerous, for my mind and body to have Spirit take over my body for an hour or so. I don't feel I need to prove anything to anybody, and when I did this, I found it a little scary; I like to be in control of my readings and not have Spirit in control of me.

So when I accepted the ability to channel, I agreed to have only the angels come through to me to fill my mind with beautiful thoughts and words. I never had a specific angel speak to me; I know when angelic energy is near, and so I called them my angels of light!

When angels are around, the energy that enters into the room is that of pure beauty! You feel ... well, I can't really express how you feel! You feel like you have been touched by something other than pure love. I also seem to get an enormous amount of energy flowing through me, almost like I have had some caffeine. This is why I only drink decaffeinated coffee.

When the angels wanted me to write something, it was never planned. So I learned very quickly to keep a small recorder with me or a pen and paper that would allow me to start channeling the divine message I would say. And I say *divine* literally! I would see beautiful purple and blue orbs, indicating to me that the angels were near, and I would write. The following is one of my previously channeled writings.

November 9th, 2010

From Marnie Hill – Spirit Wellness Inc.

As I became aware that it was time for a channeled writing, I was taking a nice leisurely walk within the park. As I was walking, I felt a huge energy shift and time stood still. As I walked and tried to make sense of this energy shift, I asked, "Who or what sends this message?"

"We do. We are the ones that reside around all of you. We are within the trees, the sky, and the ground, above all and within all. We are the life spirits of unifications and deliverance; we are the messengers from all the divine beings of light. The change that many are experiencing upon this time is also known as the unwinding. The fear that many are experiencing is the tailspin of the heart's rotation. Many already know where this comes from. Look deep inside; judgment is only a fragment of the thread that desperately wants to be unsown from within. Do not worry, though. We are present today more than ever before and are increasing.

The forces of love reside within, beside, above, as well as below. This is not something that can be taken away; this is your gift, God's gift to you. In desperate hours, one must not feel afraid, for the light is upon all of you. Please accept our gifts of Gratitude, for we need you as much as you need us. When you stand still and tall and spread your wings (arms), what do you see? We see the cross, and so should all of you.

All of you represent freedom, eternal life, gratification, unification, universal forgiveness, and love." ~The angels.

Channeling is simply getting in touch with your higher self and with the spiritual energy that is around you and willing to provide you with information. It's not mediumship or talking to the dead; it's simply being a conduit for spiritual energy to deliver written or verbal messages. No validation is required, and the information may not be specific either; it's all about love. So my journey of channeling and being a writer began; however, the channeling would quickly direct me to my true calling once again — that of being a medium! See, the other side was still preparing me and helping me build my confidence and courage.

During this time I would begin to have clients coming in for coaching, healings, and readings, and everything seemed to be going great; but I wasn't following my true calling: talking to the Afterlife. I was still afraid, and so I focused my energy on my angel readings.

During my angel readings, loved ones would come through and provide me with so much information. However, I tried to fight it, and I felt like I didn't want to let anyone know this was really who I was. The whole thing became so overwhelming that I had to eventually come to terms with my gift and once and for all put the cards away.

My spirit guide told me I only needed the cards in the beginning so I would feel more relaxed; this was to allow the transition of the spirit world to genuinely emerge with me, without my becoming fearful once again.

Remember, earlier in this book, I was so afraid of some of the information that could come forward that it took me many years to come to terms with the idea that everything would be okay. However, everything I was going through was taking a toll on me, and I began feeling unwell again.

At this time, I began to increase my knowledge and usage of crystals, and I was amazed at how much better I felt. Gemstones can be used in healing all parts of a person's life. Gemstones and crystals can help draw out negative energy that resides within your auric field (aura). Clear quartz is a stone that I use frequently. I would put a specific crystal under my pillow at night, wear crystals, and put them into the bath with me. I would also lay the crystal on each one of my chakras, do self-healing, and use the power of prayer. I noticed I began to feel better, and at the same time, I noticed my abilities were becoming much stronger. I was healing. My abilities were becoming so strong that it scared me. I began to astral-travel at night again. I did notice that Spirit was very careful not to overload me in any way with information or spiritual happenings.

One night my youngest son was having trouble sleeping, so I decided that instead of keeping everyone up all night, I would sleep in his room. I seemed to fall asleep fairly quickly, and it was definitely a deep sleep. One time during the night, I thought I was awakening, only to find myself drifting and landing in what seemed like another time. A man and woman were standing there, wearing all white, and everything around me seemed at the time to have a clear whitish colour; there was some blue, and of course the people looked very real. I remember how I felt so comfortable with them, yet I had a huge feeling of respect for them too. I would find out later that these two souls were my teachers on the other side and that they would teach me various lessons throughout my journey.

On the first occasion, I remember them teaching me how to take the light that surrounded me, wrap it into an energy ball with my hands, and dedicate a colour and a prayer within each ball I made. I would then place the balls on various areas of my body. It seemed that within this lesson, quickness was a virtue. I had to learn quickly how to draw this energy and place it on a physical form or a spiritual form. My task seemed to be a little overwhelming, and I remember being worried about leaving my son behind. My beautiful light teachers quickly reassured me that he was fine; in fact, they said, "Look to your right, Marnie. You can see him." They were right; it was like I had a thin veil surrounding me, but I could see him. I still hesitated and insisted that I must be able to check for myself. They said yes, and within a second, it felt like I literally gently fell back into the bed. I checked on him to see if he was in fact still breathing, and then quickly it seemed like I was transported back, and the teaching continued. I was told that everything they were teaching could help me and help others too. When I awoke in the morning, I really was unsure if I had astral-travelled or if I had dreamed it. It would be almost a year later when I would once again astral-travel and learn from these beings of light.

At this point, I was working with one of my clients. During coaching and helping her, I was also receiving divine guidance. When she came into a reading, I saw a little boy close to her in spirit form, and he was smiling. He would disappear once in a while, then come back during our sessions. I asked her if she had lost a child previously or if she had aborted a child. I knew from my guidance that this was not a guide but a family member. She broke down and said yes, she'd had an abortion and didn't know who the father was. This was causing turmoil within her. I asked if it would help if I described this boy. She said yes, so I did. She knows now which man fathered this child, and she learned through our sessions how to embrace his energy to release the negative memory to heal the past.

During this time frame, working with this specific client, many spiritual changes would happen to me. Still working part-time in the evenings and working with my company, I came home one night, and as I opened the door, I felt an enormous amount of energy within my home. I thought maybe my husband was up, but he wasn't. So I got a glass of water and headed downstairs to the computer. As I started the computer, I had an overwhelming desire to shut the computer off and go back upstairs. My husband always left the stove light on for me when I worked evenings, so as I was walking up the stairs, I could see the light from the stove. I had just turned off the basement light. To my wonder, I looked over to the left of me and saw a lady sitting at the table. It was my mother! Her eyes looked huge, and her body seemed slightly translucent. Her head moved, and she looked at me. My immediate response was to put my hands out to her and say, "White-light me, angels!" And poof, she was gone! I still remember exactly how she looked, and of course it took me at least five hours that night to go to bed. I was in shock, as this was so unexpected. I remembered the time when I had felt this energy feeling before — it was the same feeling

I'd had when I saw my father so many years ago. So much seemed to be happening that it would take me some time to realize the messages that were coming through for me.

I shouldn't have been afraid, but it prepared me for what was to come later in my life. I did get another opportunity to see her once more.

During this time I learned to embrace my outer visions again (my clairvoyance). It became easier to "see" outer images or Spirit. It was interesting — I noticed that my abilities were stronger on some days than on others. I have been told from the spirit world that this is normal in the beginning of acceptance, and it's all part of the process; today all is balanced, and Spirit knows exactly when I am ready to go to work.

At one point in one of my prayers and meditations, I would ask my angels and guides to show themselves to me, but another event would happen before I could actually see them with my physical eyes.

One morning while I was making my son's bed, I saw a white figure come out of my room and make its way down the stairs and then disappear! This time I wasn't scared; I think I was being prepared for something once more.

One evening while I was asleep, I woke up around 1:00 a.m. and felt a presence in my room. As I looked over at the armoire, I saw an image of a man coming to life. It was the spirit guide that I saw frequently in my inner vision. The image turned into my guardian angel Isabelle, and then I saw an eagle; the images rotated again and then disappeared.

This was one of those evenings when my husband was downstairs watching TV. I went down to see him so I could share my excitement. I sat down and told him what had happened. He looked a little nervous and said, "I'm okay with what you do. Just make sure nothing starts flying around in this house and no bad energy comes in either, Marnie!" I told him this would not be a problem; I work closely with the angels. Well, spirit visitations would increase — not only were my other family members visiting me, but spirits from other readings would begin to show up even before my angel readings. When I did start my angel readings, Spirit began to make its presence very well known. It was then when I put my cards away; I could never read from them anyway. I had such a difficult time reading them, as loved ones were always coming through trying to talk to me, and I kept shutting the door on them. I felt like I was trying to ignore them; sorry, Spirit! I did this because I was afraid — afraid of my gift. I was afraid to connect with the other side, because I ended up knowing too much about the other person and those people who were connected to me. It was always so overwhelming for me, and I didn't want to know when someone was going to die, but the spirit world was very persistent, so I made a pact with the Afterlife.

I will provide messages for the Afterlife; however, I want only important information to come through for the individual — information that will provide this world and my clients with healing and comfort. Guess what? They agreed! I am so glad I surrendered to Heaven, as my life has never been the same; it's been far happier and more fulfilled.

WARNINGS FROM THE AFTERLIFE

At one point in my journey I noticed that I was simply not getting any better with my stomach problems, and perhaps it was time to realize I needed more help; so off to the specialist I went.

One doctor wanted to give me a hysterectomy. In my dismay, I agreed, feeling nervous and downright terrified. I kept getting the same reoccurring dream. I would be lying in the hospital bed, and another manifestation of me would come up to the bed. I would be looking down at myself and seeing the pain I was in. I would look at my chart and see all the prescriptions I was put on after the surgery.

At that time an older lady would come up to me and say, "The operation shouldn't be done, Marnie. Look, look what will happen to you." Then she would lead me into a room where a number of people were sitting on a couch in a circle; there were at least eight or so other people, all older women.

These very concerned ladies were telling me about their experiences of having had a hysterectomy when they were alive and saying that I didn't need one. The pain I was experiencing was not detrimental to my health, and this experience was all a part of my soul's journey. Well, you can imagine how I felt; I was confused and a little scared to tell anyone about these dreams. The dreams came almost every night until I cancelled my appointment; then they stopped. However, the recurring dream situation still wasn't over.

The spirit world provides us with warnings all the time. Remember when I was told to change lanes while driving down the highway? I have also been told not to order a specific food, not to go out at a specific time, and not to engage in specific relationships, and to look at something on the Internet at a specific time. The hardest part, though, is actually following through and listening to the world of Spirit regarding these matters. Sometimes my own ego gets the best of me, and I refuse to listen to my inner voice or that of my guides, which always results in my life being filled with chaos. I am sure my guides and angels have shaken their heads and wondered what it would take to get my attention. I guess I have been a little bit of a rebel that way, especially earlier in my life. They never stop trying, and Spirit always forgives.

Angels just don't show up to save your life or to send you warnings; they also show up to provide validation, reassurance, and love.

After my first son was born, I was feeling a little depressed about the way I looked and was worried about being a good mom. I was a new mother who had no parents alive or guidance that I felt I could trust to help me with my new and exciting path. Not to mention, I had gained so much weight through the pregnancy, and was having difficulty with losing it. I was beginning to let the situation get the best of me. One evening I decided to go out to the mall with my son. I stopped in front of a clothing store, sat down, and daydreamed about wearing a size 4 again. All of a sudden, out of nowhere, a man appeared and sat down beside me. He was a very gentle and kind looking older man. As he looked at my son, he said what a beautiful little boy I had. My son smiled like he always did when he was a baby. I said thank you to the man. He then said, "I can't believe how happy this baby is! He is a good baby, isn't he?" I told him he was very good, and I felt very blessed. The man proceeded to say, "You know his happiness has everything to do with you. You are a great mother. You are doing a really good job — that's why he is so happy!" I looked at the man and said thank you. It was just what I needed to hear. As the man left, I looked into the stroller and smiled at my son. It was a quick second or so, and then I looked up to watch the man walk away; but he was nowhere in sight. I really believe this was an angel sent to me, to provide me with some love and reassurance — something that I desperately needed that evening.

It was two years later when I would once again seek the advice of the physician, and we agreed to do a laparoscopy since I was still having pain. Keep in mind, I had let up on the gemstone healing, which I had been doing every night, and started back on one coffee a day (I have learned my lesson today; no caffeine, please). It was about three weeks before the surgery when I came down with a really bad cold — the worst I had ever had. My EKG, done prior to the surgery, would have a "blip" in it, too. However, I was advised not to worry about it. Confused? Me, too! And so was my husband. It was mentioned to me that perhaps something was wrong with the machine and not wrong with my heart. I asked my family doctor to take another one before my surgery, just in case. It came back normal. I really wanted to make sure I had all my ducks in a row and that nothing was terribly wrong with my heart. I was very fearful, based on what I had previously experienced when I went skiing a couple of years prior.

So it would come to the final dreaded day of my surgery. I wasn't too happy about the environment they had me in, either. No private room, and the waiting room was filled with people who were waiting to have their own surgery; they were telling stories about others who had died in surgery! I kept moving around in the waiting room to find a place where I could relax. Even though I tried hard to protect myself, I could feel Spirit everywhere! My face was so hot, and I couldn't seem to relax. I psychically knew there were spirits in the waiting room that had indeed died in that hospital; I could feel it, I could hear them, and it was making me feel even more uncomfortable.

It would be in this surgery when I would have another astral-travelling experience. This one was different. I remember the anesthesiologist putting something into my arm, and I was out. From my time in surgery, I don't actually remember anything — just my astral-travelling. I awoke to find myself in a beautiful, warm, sunny place, and as I looked around, I noticed I had a large number of people circling me. They all seemed so familiar, and they looked all the same, except for one individual. I would ask this beautiful entity (or angel — I'm not sure, but I had seen her before, so I chose to speak to her) where I was and why was I there. She responded by saying, "My dear child, your soul doesn't need to feel or experience the pain your body is enduring at this time." Then she said, "Don't worry. It won't be long, and you will be back in your body." As I stood and tried to look around, I saw this large, beautiful ball. It was as big as a sun; it was pink, white, yellow, and luminescent. It seemed like I was being guarded at this time by this light. I looked over and saw other people wearing the same clothing as me. Some were lying down on what looked like sand, and others were standing, looking directly at the beautiful ball of light. I remember looking at it and feeling mesmerized; I was drawn to it.

I spoke up again, asking, "What are all these other people doing?"

She replied clearly, "My angel, they are waiting! Waiting to wake up from surgery or waiting to cross over into the light."

Everything felt so peaceful and so familiar in a strange sort of way. As I awoke from my anesthetic, the nurse was screaming at me to breathe, and I remember thinking, *Why on earth is she yelling at me?* I was in this beautiful place, but the anesthesiologist kept telling me to breathe or he was going to have to put a tube down my throat. I remember trying to breathe, but I couldn't yet; I felt so much at peace, and I just wanted this feeling of peace to last forever. Once I began to breathe, I remember the anesthesiologist asking me if I knew where I was. I said I think I'm in the Bahamas! He said I was under some bright lights, and then I remember asking him where all the people went. Suddenly, I felt it was time to stop talking, because I had experienced something incredible and no one was going to understand at that moment.

However, my physical body reacted to the anesthesia, and my heart rate wasn't regular. At one point, when my heart was pounding, I remember praying to God and thanking him for the wonderful life and family I had. I prayed to him again that my journey wasn't finished and to please take care of me. As my heart rate started returning to normal, I felt a beautiful presence next to me; I could only see a white outline, but the feeling brought me back to my childhood. I knew then that my mother's spirit was on my right and my father's spirit was on my left. I felt so warm and comfortable, and I heard my mother's voice say everything was okay. So, needless to say, I relaxed and waited for the whole physical ordeal to be over, knowing that I would, indeed, be home again.

The next day I arrived at home, but I wasn't feeling well at all. When I walked through the door with my husband and kids, I heard, "She's home, she's okay!" The energy that I felt in the home was so overwhelming. It wasn't just the energy from my children. The house seemed to be filled with souls from the Afterlife congratulating me for coming home. The voices I heard were from Heaven. So I headed up to bed, and as soon as I lay down, I saw my guardian angel again with my *physical eyes*. This was the same angel I had seen when I was astral-travelling at the hospital and the same one I had seen in my meditations before. But as clear as day, she radiated a beautiful light that surrounded her and exuded from within her. I was amazed at what I saw, and I knew all would be fine.

The next day when I awoke, I realized the power that each one of us carries within us. I had achieved astral-travelling, had had an out-of-body experience, and had heard of near-death experiences, but I hadn't heard or ever experienced anything like this before. From my experience, it seems to me that when the soul doesn't need to experience the pain, the soul goes into a holding place of sorts — a waiting place — until it needs to go back into the physical body. This whole experience was life-altering for me, and it was another experience for me to maneuver through to make sure I listened to my own warning signs, to my intuition, and to Spirit. We still didn't find out what was causing me so much pain; perhaps it was some scar tissue from a previous surgery, but today I'm as good as new!

If I don't feel comfortable about taking something or doing something that can affect my physical body, I now listen to the messages my body is giving me, to my intuition, to the other side, and to the logic of healing. This wasn't something new for me, so I really don't know why I had such a hard time with it; it shows you the importance of believing in yourself and having positive people who surround you, guide you, and support you.

Sometimes we get so focused on the drama in our lives and in everyone else's that we forget to listen to the messages that are surrounding us and are found within us. How can you hear Spirit if you are too busy texting or being drawn to the chaos within your and others' lives? It just can't happen.

I do know that each and every experience I had to endure brought me closer to God and to the spirit world. I think the Afterlife was trying pretty hard to convince me that there was more to what I was seeing and that I had the ability to communicate with the angels and with the dead.

To date I have done thousands of readings, and the information that comes through cannot be made up! I don't even know the people who sit within my individual or group readings, yet I provide them with verifiable information that no one would know about. Believe me, when I do a reading, I am humbled and touched by God each and every time.

God speaks to all of us through our hearts and minds. If your heart is riddled with hate, betrayal, anger, and mistrust, he has a hard time reaching you, and you will have a hard time hearing him.

Your loved ones will send you warnings, too, and you may even have dreams about something that is about to occur yet have no idea how you know. This is normal and can also be called *premonition*. When I was young, I received premonitions frequently, and I still do today.

One morning I woke up and said to my husband, "Not all is well within the world; something is going to happen, and it's going to happen around water! A lot of people are going to be hurt!" Well, we don't live near water, so I wasn't too sure where this was going to take place; I knew it was far. Within 24 hours, a hurricane hit China! I couldn't have done anything about it; that one was pretty much up to Mother Earth! This feeling or energy was so different; I hadn't felt it before. My guides told me the feeling I was having was coming from my empathic abilities. I was actually feeling and seeing the pain that was about to enter into this world. I have learned over the years to identify and understand the different energies that are in the spirit world and in our own world.

WHAT HAPPENS WHEN WE DIE

When I was a child, I always said, "Wouldn't it be great if when you die, God gives you the gift to visit, see, and help your family on the other side?" I was only 7 then, when I spoke about this, as I knew my mom was watching over me — no one is ever alone.

My guides have told me that when we die, we are never alone. Each one of us is walked to the other side with our guides and angels, and we get to meet loved ones who have passed over before we enter into Heaven. Once we have entered the gates, we are immediately brought forward into a life review. After the life review where we have had an opportunity to explain ourselves, we are ready for our own individual healing levels. With each level, if we have hurt someone, we will feel their pain and we will need to come up with a reason and learn how we could have done things better.

One evening as I fell into a deep sleep, I remember awakening only to remember something that felt like a dream. When I travel, I fall into a sleep where my husband says I don't move at all and he can barely hear me breathe. This night, I ended up in a place that looked like a hall, and my guide was waiting at the front door to see me. I asked why I was here, and he said he needed to show me something that would help me on my journey. As we entered this hall, there seemed to be many different rooms, but the rooms were not closed in; it was almost like there was a thin glass wall before each one of them.

I saw a marriage ceremony taking place, and I asked my guide, Joe, what was happening; he told me that they were celebrating their anniversary. I remember looking at him and saying, "This isn't a dream, is it?"

He smiled and said no. He said, "Marnie, I have brought you to a place where people have a chance to learn, heal, and ask for forgiveness for the sins that they created within the physical world." He said that everything we do and say is actually recorded into a hall of records, and we are judged at the time of our deaths.

You can come here and either celebrate or take action and ask for forgiveness. So as we entered into another room, I saw a little boy celebrating his birthday. In another room, a man was talking and people were gathered around listening; he was crying and asking for forgiveness. At this moment, I began to feel a little uncomfortable as we began to walk down the hall into another room. I looked at Joe and said, "Can I please go? I don't want to see this." As soon as I said that, two females appeared next to Joe; all three of them were with me and said I had nothing to fear — that no one could hurt me here and that I was protected.

I entered into a room where another man was crying uncontrollably; he had chains around his body and was chained to a chair. The people around him were angry; he had hurt many people in his lifetime and was going to have to experience the pain that each person had endured — the pain he had brought on. I took a deep breath, and then the three of them took me aside. Joe looked at me. "Marnie, everyone's judgment is based on what they do with their life on planet earth."

He continued, "Each soul has its own journey, and I know you can feel its pain, but you cannot hold onto another person's pain. You must let other people's pain go. It is time to move forward with your life and let go of the worry about other people. Let God take care of it so you can do your job on earth."

I remember starting to leave this place, and within a second it felt like I was plopped back onto my bed. I opened my eyes. Still not feeling very comfortable about what I had seen, I explained it to my husband the next day. He really is an angel who has been sent to me, to help me on this journey and for me to help him on his. When you become aware and open up to the possibilities, God, spirit guides, and your deceased loved ones will help you on your journey; they come in a dream, through astral-travelling, or by sending you little messages. That the spirit world is a smile or a thought away can bring you an enormous amount of peace.

Spirit will also seek you out to deliver or experience something that will either help you or help someone on the other side. I personally needed to see and hear this message from my guide. I had been so worried and wrapped up with some outside family situations that were happening, I began to concentrate more on fixing something I couldn't fix instead of focusing on a place where I could help, as was my calling.

One of the questions I am asked regularly is if someone will come through if they were not a believer in mediums or in Heaven when they were alive. It's a good question, and believe me, when we pass over, everyone is going to get a big surprise knowing it's okay to seek the assistance of a medium, and yes, Heaven is for real! After all, mediums are here to help you and your loved ones through the process of grief, and Heaven is actually home.

There is always someone who is in shock when a loved one who didn't believe in mediums or in Heaven comes through. Death doesn't mean the stop of communication or healing; it simply means a different form of communication. Your loved ones also speak whatever language the medium speaks; communication is universal, so the messages are adaptive to the medium, and after the communication is done, your loved ones return to Heaven. It's that simple.

I have been told from the other side that our deaths are predetermined before we arrive in this world. Some souls are only meant to live a short time, while others live longer. I have mentioned this before. You do get opportunities to extend your life, if you listen and follow through with what is required for your mind and body to receive optimal healing and health. And sometimes death is just meant to be. The soul is ready to move on into the Afterlife, whether we like it or not. You are not being punished, and neither is the person who dies; the soul is simply ready for Heaven. This can be difficult to understand, as so many people feel angry when another person has passed. It's important to remember, though, that we are all here to learn something about love.

SUICIDE AND THE SOUL

I feel it's important to talk about suicide at this time. Being a survivor of a family member who committed suicide, and being a medium, I feel qualified to speak on this subject. Please remember, I am not disrespecting any religion. I am merely stating facts that I have experienced in hopes of helping another person who has also lost a loved one through suicide.

Earlier in the book, I spoke about my mother, who committed suicide, and how I would always tell people she had passed away in a car accident. I did this because I was afraid of judgment. It was sad that I was afraid of what people would think of me at such a young age, from grade two forward. My mother's suicide was a very traumatic event in my life and in other people's lives too. Many things happened the evening before she actually took her own life, which would forever affect the impact her suicide had on me.

The evening on which my mother committed suicide was the evening my father had gone out to do some work with the business he was in. That evening, they had both been arguing over various things, and my mom wasn't acting normal at all. She seemed confused and very mad. My father left. My sibling and I were instructed to take a bath. During this time, we heard an odd sound, as if my mother was busy doing something in the living room. We called out to her to rinse our hair like she always did, but she didn't answer. Shortly after this, we both smelled smoke. I got out of the tub as quick as I could and saw my mother attempting to light the house on fire by first trying to light the jackets in the closet. I ran back into the bathroom, and we both quickly got dressed and ran out to where my mother was. I tried to get a pot of water to put out the fire, but she kept finding something to light. I was panicking and asking her to stop, but she didn't, and she seemed like she was in her own world, like she couldn't even hear me. Both my sibling and I ran to the neighbor's house, and they called the fire department. My mother came back for us, and she was furious. I knew this wasn't my mother talking. She seemed different. She told everyone that the fire was out and it was okay to come home.

After she brought us back to the house, she took us into the bathroom and started yelling at us, telling us we should always listen to her and we should have never left the house. She closed the door and left. I opened the door and quietly went into the hallway. I could see her reach into a drawer in the kitchen to pull out a wooden spoon, which was what we got spanked with when we were bad. Well, my mother didn't get a wooden spoon like I thought; I had only assumed that's what she was going to do. Instead she pulled out a knife. I saw the whole thing; we needed to leave immediately, but she took us back into the bathroom. Before we could get away, my mom cut me on the wrist and my sibling a couple of times on the arm. Terrified, we finally got away from her and ran to the house next door for safety. We were barefoot, crying, and running in the snow on a cold winter evening.

As I ran out of the house, I looked back and I saw my mom's face; it was then I realized she had just noticed what she had done. When she had reached into the drawer to get the wooden spoon, she wasn't looking at what she pulled out. Her face was white, and she was in shock when she looked at the knife and realized what had just taken place — cutting me and my sibling. That was the last time I saw my mother, and I feel she committed suicide because of her own emotional state and what she thought she had done to us. I do think what she did was an accident, **not** premeditated. She was sick. Perhaps she couldn't live with it — I am not sure. All I know is what I remember and what my guides have told me about that night. So you can see why

I chose to keep it quiet. Not too many people would understand what had taken place or why; I don't like pity, and judgment is unnecessary.

Once I did tell the story, I had to live with comments such as, "You can't possibly be normal with something like that happening to you" throughout my life from people who were judgmental and uncaring. I needed to learn how to move on, and I did. Besides, I talk to people in the Afterlife. How normal is that?

Too many times, I have had people ask me what happened to my wrist, and instinctually I know they think I tried to harm myself. They just give me that strange, sad look with their eyes that says something like, "How could you?" I have never even been close to thinking of ending my life — not ever. I had to dream up another story so everyone would understand and basically leave me alone regarding the scar on my wrist. I used to tell people I had fallen off my bike when I was 7 and my wrist landed on some glass. The cut was so deep I needed stitches. The scar on my wrist frequently reminds me of one of the biggest and most hurtful battles in my life — a battle that I survived. I was meant to make it, and I only wish my mother could have as well.

Just because someone has had some difficult moments in life doesn't mean there is anything wrong with the person. Sometimes people are in the wrong place at the wrong time, and let's face it, perhaps their soul needed to experience something that could help them or others, only in a different time. Even though so much of that traumatic event took place in the bathroom, today it's one of my favorite places of relaxation. Candles, soft music, and a nice warm bath! A soul healed!

I never think about that night except when I have something that is too tight on my wrist or if someone questions me. Anytime I have something restricting that area, other than a watch, my wrist and some fingers seem to go numb and tingly, and sometimes, but not all the time, I get memories of what happened that evening. I don't have any feelings or emotions attached to the memory, so I know I have already been healed. This also reinforces something I have learned long ago. Your body remembers, and even scars can hold a memory imprint; that's why healing your past is so important. Many people are taught to just let it go, move on; but the reality is that you can't move on until you are healed from the incident. Time doesn't heal wounds; only healing does, and this requires commitment and movement.

I had a really close friend in grade four. Let's say her name was Veronica. Veronica and I were really close. I went to her house over lunch hour during the week. She lived a ways from me, so I never spent time on the weekends with her. Veronica's mom was very religious, and I could respect that at an early age. However, I also could tell she seemed uncomfortable with me, especially when she found out that neither I nor my family were going to church at this time. I really didn't pay much attention to it; I just remained very quiet within her presence.

One day, I felt that I wanted to tell Veronica the truth about my mom. I had been keeping this inside for a long time, and I felt I could trust her. I wasn't prepared at all for what was to happen. So one day while at break time, I told Veronica the truth about my mom — how she had committed suicide. I told her my mom wasn't well and that, yes, my father ended up dating my babysitter. She looked at me, and I could see her heart was open, and she thanked me for telling her the truth. I felt really good about it until the next day.

Every morning I would see her, and we would talk around our lockers. Veronica's mom had driven her to school that day. When Veronica arrived, she wouldn't look at me at all. This was not normal behavior for her. At break I asked her what was wrong, and she couldn't tell me. At lunch, I spent the hour alone; Veronica was nowhere in sight. The next day, I came up to her and asked her again what was wrong. She told me she had spoken with her mom about me and told her mom everything about my mother and my life. Veronica said her mom told her I was evil, that my mom was in Hell and my father was going to go to Hell, too. And maybe even me! She had been instructed to never speak with me again, and if she did, she would be grounded for a very long time. The next year Veronica was moved to a private school. Suicide hurts; it hurts the souls of the living and of the dead.

I have met a lot of souls in the Afterlife who have committed suicide, and they all seem to feel the same way about what they did. They are sorry and are aware that this action was something they shouldn't have done and apologize for the pain they have caused everyone.

I have been told numerous times from the other side that all is forgiven, especially when we have a mental illness. When mental illness leads one to commit suicide, it means the soul is in trouble and is not able to get back on its path. Remember the life review I spoke of earlier? Well, it comes into play no matter how you died, so it is up to God to decide what level your soul will remain on to heal. Your guides are very much a part of this decision, as are you. Once the decision has been made, you will go to a specific level of healing before you ever reincarnate and are born again. There is no time in the spirit world, so years may feel like only days. No one ever reincarnates into another life until his or her current healing is complete.

It took me many years to be able to connect with my mother in the spirit world. In fact, the first time she tried to communicate with me was when I had my second child. I always felt her presence, but it seemed like we couldn't connect properly. Perhaps both of us were not ready, and perhaps she was too busy going through the levels of her own healing in Heaven. After all, she is one of my helpers today from the Afterlife, and I can imagine one's spirit needs to be really healed from God to be able to do this type of work to help the living.

Part of a soul's healing may include a medium. The first and foremost reason we have mediumship abilities is for healing, and this should be at the forefront of every medium's mind.

When a soul comes through and it wants to heal its life circumstance with a client, the soul can put a healing symbol over the client's heart chakra, and I know we are going to have an intense reading ahead. After validation has been brought forward, the soul begins the healing by talking about the past with information verifiable by my client. A medium can bring a soul that has passed over hours after that soul has left the physical world.

As a medium, having continuous readings from souls who have committed suicide can be very draining on my own soul; it's also both painful and healing for the client who is sitting in front of me. To avoid getting too overwhelmed, I have asked Spirit to only show me what I need to see and hear to provide enough validation for the loved ones who have survived. Seeing blood continuously, seeing a hanging or mutilation of a body — not to mention feeling the effects of a drug going through the body or feeling their mental illness — can take a toll on my emotional well-being, too! This is why I have always told people that delivering messages from the Afterlife is not to be glorified or for fun! I will talk about this more in the chapter *Are Ghosts Real?* I can tell you a couple of important details now, however. Every soul I have ever come into contact with who has died by suicide is completely aware of their actions before they pass into the light, and the remorse they feel is enormous — so much so that they want to go back, but the body has already died. I have also met souls who did not commit suicide, but all evidence pointed to it, and this can be an intense reading to say the least!

HEAVEN HAS VISITING HOURS

About six years ago, on a Friday afternoon back when I was doing some angel readings, I was still nervous about bringing *me* into the world and allowing Spirit to fully communicate with me. I was still scared, but I knew if I concentrated on what the cards were telling me and what my psychic abilities were saying, I would be okay. Spirit had a different plan for me one evening.

I received a frantic message on my voicemail from a lady saying she had planned a dinner party and that the psychic she had hired was sick; would I be able to attend? She apologized for the short notice, but of course I agreed to attend her party because those were the days when I wasn't booked two or more months in advance. I was absolutely excited, and I had no idea where this one night would end up. So I attended the "party" of eight people, meaning I was to provide eight mini-readings, which usually lasted 15–20 minutes in length for each participant.

All was going great and the guests were happy with the information, and I was feeling good, too. That's always a good sign! It was near the end of one reading that a lady came in with great energy; she had an open mind and heart! During the reading, her guides were giving so much positive information regarding her life and her future. Then a huge energy shift happened, and a little boy came into the reading. I saw his outline, and using my abilities, I connected with him telepathically. (When this happens, all logic and fear go out the window; Spirit is in the driver's seat.) I mentioned I had a small boy present, and I went into great detail about how he looked and, yes, gave information about how he died. He was sad, though, as within this message was another message that I would find the meaning of later. I told her that the boy was sad, as his grave has been forgotten, and he wished to have a memorial plaque or something. During the reading, she was looking at me with amazement and, yes, hesitation. I told her that something was odd about his death. "Do you know this boy?"

Well, the only boy she knew who looked like that and who was at that age was her cousin who had gone missing more than twenty years before. She said he was still missing. I had to tell her the bad news. "No, this boy, your cousin who has passed over, passed over shortly after he was abducted." I closed the reading immediately, as she seemed a little overwhelmed by the news. I told her that as a medium, I needed to deliver the message; she would need to decide what action she would like to move forward with and how, as where I lived, the police unfortunately did not work with psychics or mediums that I was aware of. Being a little nervous at never having had a reading like this before nor any idea what to do with it, I prayed something good would come from it.

I ended up getting an email from the grandmother of the child. She was a little furious and still in denial that her grandson may actually be gone. So I did what my guides told me to and let it go. The lady I did the reading with had another angel party; she loved them so much! Each friend would have another angel party, and with each one of those, lives were changed and healed for the better.

I had one group angel reading where I had already read for a lady; I will call her Sally for the sake of the book. When I began the reading for Sally, the same message came back as before, as she told me I had already said this before to her. However, this time the message had even more urgency than previously. I usually don't remember my readings, but this one really stuck out in my mind. Sally's guides were telling me to tell her to have her son-in-law get help with his drinking and his emotional well-being.

I am the messenger; my hands are tied after the message has been delivered. Well, that evening, she would be the one who won a free 30-minute reading with me. When I saw Sally a couple of months later, in my meditation prior to the reading, my guide told me someone close to her has passed — a male, a son.

When I went into the reading, I knew immediately it was her son in-law, the man who I was told needed to stop drinking. He was the one who had passed, and he was eager to speak with her. I was happy to inform Sally that her son-in-law was going to be a part of the reading to explain how he had passed. There was confusion if he had in fact committed suicide or not.

It was a couple of months later when the deceased's wife would come in, and we once again connected to him; this time the message was very clear and detailed, even though his wife was still very upset. He provided an enormous amount of information and validation regarding his death and the events leading up to it. As a medium, I was so pleased that I had brought closure to both of them! When the deceased gives me a nod or thumbs up, he or she is letting me know that everything is going to be okay. Being an empath can always be a difficult thing and a blessing when dealing with these types of readings. The deceased will express the deep love and the pain they have felt throughout their lives, and sometimes we get into a little thing called perceptions.

It's difficult when the loved one who has passed over expresses his or her emotional well-being and the living were not aware of what the deceased was feeling at the time when he or she was alive. I need to be really delicate on how the communication comes forward so as not to hurt anyone's feelings or cause any more heartache regarding the passing.

Those in the Afterlife get really excited and like to show me their personality before and during the reading. Believe me, Spirit uses any opportunity it can to speak with loved ones; however, I have guidelines because my family is the most important thing in my life to me, so when my kids or my husband is around, Spirit treads delicately when I am out and about doing my own thing: living!

Usually I know how intense the reading is going to be based on my body temperature. If it's an intense reading, my face seems to get flushed and I know Spirit is near, yet my hands remain frozen. If I am getting ready to do energy healing, my body gets cold and my hands heat up. However, I really never know what the reading is going to be like until I sit down in front of my clients or the group I will be reading for. Every little hint Spirit gives me (souls in the Afterlife) is here to help me with my session. It's to help my body prepare for the energy of Spirit.

I don't have to have a client show up or even book with me to receive messages from the Afterlife. One day while I was sitting at my computer, I had a boy show up. I could feel him and see his outline with my physical eyes. These images were of a little boy who recently went missing in our city, along with some of his family members. When the notice came out on the news that this boy and some of his family members were missing, within about three days he came to me. I ran outside to tell my husband that the little boy came to me and said he was dead. He explained to me that his body was not in fact in the same city. He showed me dirt and rocks, and I also felt that his leg had been hurt. I am really not sure about communication like this; when they show up out of the blue, it can be a little confusing at times — and it was only the little boy speaking to me.

Within a couple of days after my visitation, the news reported that the police were now looking at this case as a homicide and that they were searching for the bodies outside of the city. It was exactly what the boy had told me. I looked at my husband and asked what I should do. Should I call the police and try to connect with the boy in their presence? Fearful of what some people would do with the information I could provide, I decided to leave it in the hands of the police, but this action was eating away at my soul.

It was a couple of days later that I saw a friend of mine, and I couldn't keep it inside me anymore; I literally broke down in tears and told her the story. She firmly agreed with my actions. I went into a healing session with her, and the boy revisited me and said he simply knew I was a medium and could talk to the dead. He was sorry for causing me so much pain and gave me a bouquet of flowers in the form of Lego! I told him it was time for him to go to Heaven and be with his other family members, and he did. I haven't heard from him since. A week later, some family members spoke out about this little boy, and they mentioned his soft heart and how caring he was. It was just more validation from the other side — validation I needed.

Today I have an action plan in place, and when something like this happens again, this action plan will help the deceased and not put me or my family at risk of being attacked from negative people and people who are non-believers.

In another one of my medium readings, a man came through to verify that he had in fact died in a car crash; he had been drinking, and he felt horrible for what had happened. The wife, who had not been in the vehicle at the time, was in so much distress, as she and her husband had a fight before he left the house. That was the same night he would die on the highway. It was an emotional reading for sure; I knew they'd had a fight as he told me, and before the crash, he'd wanted to apologize to her to let her know that he was in fact coming home to see her. He had forgiven her and loved her so much, and he needed her forgiveness too. This reading brought so much closure to her life. Our loved ones come through to help us heal; this is why they speak from the other side.

Please keep in mind that within my readings, I only ask for a yes or a no to the validation I provided. I do not want pictures or jewelry from the deceased, and I do not ask questions, and on most occasions I don't even look at my clients. I don't want to know anything about what has happened. This ensures I receive the information directly from Spirit, not from the client's energy field or from my left brain!

I am not in charge of who comes through or shows up for a reading or even if Spirit wants to; it's all up to the spirits in Heaven. I would have to say that 95% of the time, they do show up and provide us with all sorts of information and laughter! Yes, they love to provide us with their personality; this is validation of their existence.

I find the readings that really impact me are ones when a loved one comes through to provide some intense healing, as he or she knows exactly what their loved ones need. I had a lady looking for information regarding her father; her grandmother on the other side was able to give some incredible information regarding her father's life. In fact, the grandmother showed me a book and kept turning the pages until she could show me a picture. The deceased and spirit guides usually connect with me telepathically and by using symbols or sending specific words for me to hear. Not very often do I see them physically standing beside the client, but I don't worry about it at all. Whatever Spirit needs to have happen will happen. I'm a conduit for the healing to take place.

Your loved ones, spirit guides, and angels will not reveal information that may inhibit your growth or your life path. Many times I have had people come into a reading expecting the world, and when I educate them on what really happens within a reading, they gain a different perspective on the ability — a much wiser one. It is unfortunate this gift and ability of talking to dead isn't given more positive attention. It helps so many.

I have talked a bit about my abilities to talk to the other side, but I am also a psychic. You can't be a medium and not be a psychic; it's the next level up, really!

Many times people want to hear from their loved ones but really need advice regarding their lives. I never deny Spirit communication, so no matter what type of a reading I do, Spirit is always going to show up. However, like I said before, Spirit can be really chatty and provide all sorts of information. So I felt it was important to offer two different types of readings: one reading where someone can speak with a loved one and get some healing information and then a different type of reading where a person gets some quick information and validation from loved ones but also gets some detailed information about his or her past, present, and future.

I am not a fortune teller; my gift is not to tell you about your fortune, as only you, yourself, have the ability to enhance or wreck your life. I can see future events; however, the events I see are already written on your life path, so it's okay for me to tell you what I am seeing. You, at the time, have the ability to make changes in your life if this future outcome is something you would prefer not to have happen. Or you can take the information provided and feel happy and confident on the path you are on. Or perhaps the information being provided will give you some insight on where it is you need to go.

I feel, if you want to be rich, work for it! If you want a better job, find one! If you want a husband or a wife, get into alignment in order to receive one! I always told myself I would never be one of the mediums or psychics sitting in a caravan or even a tent delivering messages, and you will never see me staring into a crystal ball or anything like that.

Even though I can get all sorts of information about your life, the information that comes through in a reading is different for everyone. It's always what you need to hear. So if you need information about your career, I can see information about upcoming job opportunities and growth; it is automatically provided to me. If you need information about your relationship, I will be provided information about your current and future relationships. I can even see the people in your life — what they look like and how they fit into your life. If you need information about your past life, that is what I will see. Whatever it is you need, the information will be provided directly to me from all sorts of different sources. It may be from your loved ones. It may come from your soul. It may come from your spirit guides or mine. And it may even come from your angels and God. I am simply a conduit for spirit energy and information that your soul would like to provide me with.

ARE GHOSTS REAL?

Unfortunately, in my earlier years, I experienced on numerous occasions things that happened that could be called a "haunting" or a "ghostly experience." I guess I could say both of my children did too; in fact, they were the ones who once brought it to my attention that perhaps something was in the house. However, ghosts are souls in Heaven.

I was doing a tremendous amount of healing on a young lady who suffered from depression. She spent most of her leisure time hanging out in bars and around people who were taking drugs and having lots of parties. During her healing, I saw her on a weekly basis in hopes of helping her move through some difficult moments. She had a lot of negative energy hanging around her — I could tell the moment I saw her — and she had one particular soul who liked to attach to her. I tried diligently to see if there was something I could do that would allow the soul to go back into the light, and he eventually did; but she needed to change her lifestyle and thought process in order for this to happen. Eventually she did, and she healed. However, within that time frame, I had two fish die, and my spider plant died. I recommend everyone have fish and spider plants in their area of healing to penetrate any negative energy; it's better than it going into you!

Even though I had cleared my home on several occasions, the energy became very dense within one particular area of the house. My children began to feel a sense of uncertainty and began to feel uneasy for a couple of days. When the kids and I were in the kitchen, we heard something like, "Go away ..." I'm not kidding! All three pairs of our eyes got wide, and I saw a black mass in the area of the sound. Well, it was a nice day, and I quickly sent the kids outside without putting fear within them, and I tried to shrug it off. I went to work on clearing and healing the space. It was an eye-opener, and from that day forward I gave strict power to my guides and angels to remove any negative energy from my home, my family, and myself any time, whenever it was needed. I'm sure they are busy healing everyone while we sleep.

I have always believed that our thoughts create our emotions, so where we live can also be a reflection of our thoughts and other people's thoughts, too. So what does that have to do with the Afterlife and your home? Quite a bit! Like I mentioned before, I do believe in dark energies and entities; however, I also know that the brighter your soul is, the more dark energies can be attracted to you. But they can't stay if you resonate at a high vibration of love — meaning if you are full of love and light, dark energy can't stay with you. However, I always need to experience everything, and even though I resonate at a high vibration level, I need to also know the truth to help me on my journey.

Every living soul wants to be loved and accepted — even the dark, but it doesn't know how. Many times a soul wants to be heard or wants to deliver a message to the homeowner or to his or her loved ones. So when this happens, many people hear noise, feel breezes in the air, walk through cold spots in the home, and so on. A poltergeist is actually very rare, and so is a possession, at least in the West, though I hear it is still around in other parts of the country. In ancient times, mental illness was considered a possession, as no one understood what was happening, and they had not yet reached a place of understanding the mind. So when I get a request to do a house clearing and blessings, I approach it very delicately, as the majority of the times it's a loved one dropping in to say hello and try to deliver a message.

One summer, my husband, kids, and I took a trip and ended up staying in a couple of hotels. We try to stay in the most comfortable yet affordable accommodations. However, my husband decided to book us at one particular hotel for one night. When we approached the hotel, I asked my husband how old this place was and why I was feeling it has been converted into a hotel from a nightclub.

My husband said it was because it was a nightclub before. I think he had visited it once or twice many, many years ago! The hotel was beautiful, and as I walked into the front door, I could feel the presence of souls in the Afterlife who were in the hotel. I could smell the residue of old cigarette smoke and alcohol; it was unpleasant, but I knew Spirit was near, so it was okay.

Late into the night — it must have been around 1:00 or 2:00 a.m., I saw a man standing over my bed. Without being scared, as I had learned no spirit can hurt me (God is always near), I said out loud, "I am on holidays, please go away! You are not welcome here." Well, he didn't leave, so I began to say the Lord's Prayer. I do this to raise my vibrational frequency and to call in my angels. Within a second, a beautiful white light appeared in the corner of the room. I heard a female voice say, "I am here to protect you. Nothing can hurt you, and I will be here all night." So feeling more comfortable, I went back to sleep, and the ghost man eventually left.

In the morning, I asked my husband exactly how many people did he think may have died in this place. He said he remembered hearing about a few. I told him I'd had the most interesting night. My son had just awakened and didn't hear my question to my husband, and I hadn't yet explained what had happened to me. My son said, "Mom, you're not going to believe what happened last night. I woke up and saw this beautiful angel in the room. It must have been really late. She was standing in the corner and said not to worry; she was here to protect us. I looked over at you, and you were fast asleep, so I went back to bed."

Looking at my husband and my sons in incredulity, I told them about my night. My husband spoke calmly. "Wow, that's incredible!" I saw happiness and excitement in my son's eyes. It's always a beautiful moment when you see your children believe in something as wonderful as God and the angels.

All morning, I was feeling a little out of sorts. I could still sense a particular spirit was very close to me, but I wasn't receiving any messages. I couldn't hear anything, and no images were coming to me; I just felt so many emotions from this spirit. So the kids helped their dad load up the bags while I was getting ready. I wanted to get the boys out of the hotel room as soon as I could.

As they made their way downstairs, I remained in the room doing my hair. When I finished my makeup, I felt a huge breeze come in, and I knew someone was going to try to communicate with me from the Afterlife. My son had been playing with a plastic belt that held some sort of toy, and it was still lying on the bed. Within a couple of seconds, that plastic belt was thrown to the ground all by itself. I strengthened my resolve, saying, "I command you to leave now." I recited the Lord's Prayer. My husband came in within minutes, and I said it was time to go. As we drove away from the hotel, I explained to my husband that there was a spirit in our room, trying to communicate with me. However, the energy from him felt angry or perhaps in some sort of emotional pain. As we drove away, I simply visualized the hotel and the room we were in and placed God's white light protection around the spirit to help him heal or to help him move towards the light.

I had been asked to do a house clearing and blessing for a lady, as she was experiencing a lot of misfortune in her life. Before I arrived at the door of her home, I could feel the energy rising within me. When she opened the door to greet me, I felt a strong energy come along with her too! We sat down at the table, and before we could go over the contract, I looked at her and said, "Your dad's here. He wants to speak with you." She agreed to the reading, so we went and began the contract and prayer.

After the messages were delivered, I cleared the house. There was absolutely nothing wrong in the house; her dad was trying to speak to her about making some life changes. Her misfortune was happening for a reason, and she needed to change her lifestyle quickly. This was a classic case of her energy interfering with the energy of her home, and her beloved dad wanted to help. It was an amazing experience. So not all spirit visitations in homes are bad, but they can be, if you let them.

This leads me to talk about a very important area: séances, Ouija boards, and speaking to spirits for fun. There is nothing fun about talking to the dead, and no one should ever approach this as being a game. Yes, I have mentioned this a couple of times throughout my book, in hopes the message is received. Evil exists; the Bible talks about it numerous times, and many other religions refer to it also. As I said before, I am not going to get into religion too much within this book, but I can see why the warning is set in place. Too many people enter into psychic or mediumship work with no prior knowledge or understanding about Spirit and the Afterlife, resulting in psychics or mediums ending up sick and even hurting the very people they want to help — their clients. If you are meant to do this work, you will know it. You will, however, be required to experience all sorts of experiences to gain knowledge about the Afterlife and Heaven. You do need to keep your wits about you and understand that this work should be taken seriously at all times.

ANGELS & SPIRIT GUIDES

Throughout this book I have spoken about God, my own spirit guides, and angels, so I want to touch a bit on this topic. I could write a whole book about it, but I think that will be for a later date.

When we are born, each one of us is appointed a guardian angel. This angel is close to the high counsel, your gate keepers, and your spirit guides. The high counsel is the controller for your contract with God. Spirit guides have been appointed to you not only by your soul before you were born but also by your guardian angel. Your guardian angel is closest to the archangels — archangels such as the Archangel Michael, Archangel Raphael, Archangel Uriel, and Archangel Gabriel (and I am sure there are many more who are closest to God).

This is how it has been referenced to me from my own spirit guides:

God

Messengers of Light (Archangels)

Angels

High Counsel — Gate Keepers

Spirit Guides

The Afterlife

Humans on Earth

The archangels are messengers of light who are available to anyone who calls upon them. Their main purpose is to help God, this planet, and all the people who live within it.

Your own guardian angel has been appointed to you from God and is available to you if you are in a life-or-death situation.

When I was in the hospital during my operation, I did get to see my guardian angel. However, I couldn't see all of her. What I did see looked like it was pure light, yet she was close enough for me to see her face and feel her presence of love. She needed to show me the other side and show herself to me again when I was home. I was told that I was okay and that she needed me to relax so my body could relax and my heart rate could return to normal. It was very important that she help me during this time.

A spirit guide is a soul who has been appointed to you from birth and will remain with you and help you pass over into the light. Their main function is also to ensure you are living your life to the fullest and following your soul contract. Your spirit guides converse with your guardian angel, with gate keepers, and with the high counsel. Most spirit guides have lived before within other lifetimes but not necessarily on the same planet; they can be extraterrestrial too! I have no idea on how I connect with the Afterlife, with my spirit guides, or with any of the spiritual realms. They simply come to me and show up every time I am ready to go to work and do a reading or need help and guidance within my own life.

The high counsel is the being I saw within one of my evening travels. These beings are in place to ensure you are working well with your spirit guide and following your soul contract. They are the ones who can change your contract for you when it is requested from your spirit guides and the angels. Your gate keeper is exactly what it sounds like; it is also your protector and the keeper of your contract. Did you know that not everyone can gain access to your records? They will not have that opportunity if their intention is not of the highest light.

I have been told by my guides that if another person's intention, such as one who works within this industry, isn't good, then they don't want to help. If someone is in this business for glory or for malicious reasons, he or she will not be able to talk to the other side or even have access to your records. He or she may be able to read your energy, but the majority of the time, it won't be correct because that person is feeding off of his or her own fear and insecurities. There is a higher order with all of this, and God, your guides, and angels will protect you if you let them!

I have found that meditation is always helpful if you need to make a connection with the higher realms when they are not appearing when requested. Remember, just because you can't see or hear them doesn't mean they are not with you; sometimes they need to be quiet so you can grow.

My male guide, "Joe," has had a previous life with me, and so did my other spirit guide, "Isabelle." Both of them were healers in previous lives, and Joe was considered a saint when he was alive.

Spirit guides and angels are not big on names. Names are used for identification purposes within our lives and are a requirement for the ego. There is no ego on the other side, so it took me some time to get their true names. I know Joe isn't my guide's true name, but I call him that. Perhaps his real name would be too difficult for my mind to accept!

Our loved ones can become our guides on the other side, too. However, I have been told from the Afterlife that in order for a loved one to become a guide, that person must first go through his or her own healing. There is no time in Spirit; days can feel like months, and months, like years. Our loved ones do get the opportunity to drop in from time to time to see you and say hello. This is how the dead can provide mediums with so much information; they are telling us what they have seen. Sometimes they can stay for a couple of minutes; other times they can stay for hours. Again, it all depends on what level someone is in with their healing and how long their own guides and angels allow them to stay.

When I connect with people who have recently passed on to the other side, their energy isn't completely grounded yet for human communication. They can communicate; however, they may fade in and out, until they get grounded with their new set of legs in Heaven. Communication also depends on your soul's desire to do so. Sometimes the dead need help from the medium's spirit guide to help them communicate with their loved ones. Our angels and guides are always with us and ready to help when needed or when called upon.

When I was little, before my mother passed, every Sunday I went to a small church in our community. It always felt safe there, like I was home. The only information I received at home that I can remember was the importance of prayer and how to pray with rosaries. This came from my mother. The desire to go to church was so strong, I walked many times on my own when I was only 5. It was a small town!

Even today I am fascinated by churches. When I visited Paris, I went to the Sacred Heart Church, and I didn't want to leave! The energy there was incredible. I felt the power of God. There are no words that can describe those feelings I had. They were so intense, so holy, I felt like I could drop to my knees and pray. These emotions have been related to many of my past lives. I have a spirit guide who was a saint in his past life, so no wonder I am drawn to churches; it's part of my energy and my soul.

In my readings, I always bring in the power of God and angelic light, and I request that God and Archangel Michael take guard and surround me and my client with the highest light of protection, to ensure no dark energies come through into the reading or into my life or my client's life.

I have many people who come into my reading saying, "I am a Christian, and I don't believe in this stuff." When I ask, "Then why would you come?" they say they need more guidance in their life, need to heal from a loss, and felt drawn to attend a reading. I think deep within their souls, they know it's okay and that perhaps it was a higher power calling them to seek guidance; this can be from God, our spirit guides, angels, or our loved ones. Remember, help always arrives when asked.

One day I had a friend come down and visit me; it was the babysitter! I hadn't seen her for a while, and I wanted to connect with my mother in spirit, to see if she was okay that I was in fact connected to her. For some reason, I needed my mother to be okay with it. So before the babysitter was to arrive, I told my mother what was happening and said if she could send me a message from the other side that all was okay, that would really help me.

On the second day after the babysitter arrived, we decided to go shopping, and I really wanted to take her to a specific mall. Knowing this was far from my home and time was of the essence, I really wanted to take her there and to a specific store. I told her that she would love the clothes in this store, and I knew she would. However, while we were in the mall, I wanted to get to the store and not look at the other stores she wanted to. I felt a little selfish, but I couldn't help the urgency I was feeling.

So we went into the store, and immediately I took her to one specific area. I felt like I was being directed to a specific place. She followed, and I stopped suddenly at a rack that had beautiful jackets and ponchos. As soon as I stopped, I saw my mother within my inner vision and sensed her sprit. The babysitter looked at me and said, "Marnie who does this coat remind you of?" I had no clue. I didn't know how to answer because I saw my mother when we stood by the coats! A little confused by the question, I answered and said the only person I have in my mind is my mother, and then the babysitter went white as a ghost and said, "Oh my God! As soon as you brought me to this area, I kept seeing your mom in my mind!"

Well, I never told the babysitter about what I had requested from my mom before she arrived, and we never usually talk too much about her, and then this happened! This was the sign my mother could send me, to let me know she was okay with everything. The babysitter needed to experience my mother's communication to also receive the message, and both of our spirit guides were facilitating the journey. Don't tell me we're not getting help from the other side!

In one of my group readings I was doing a reading for a lady who was struggling with a serious physical illness. During my reading, Jesus showed up! I am not kidding you! I felt a little nervous in telling her this, but I did, and then I told her what he was telling me! I told her, "Jesus is telling me to tell you not to lose faith and that he has not left you. He is always standing with you, even on this journey." He told me she had lost her faith in him. I asked her what that meant to her, and she told me that morning she was so mad that she was not getting better that she asked Jesus why he wasn't helping her. She asked him if she did something wrong to get this disease. Well, the message was delivered that day, and she knew Jesus in fact never left her. He said so through his message.

I have been told many times from my own spirit guides that the angels and all higher-level spirits always let our loved ones speak first during a reading, as they know this is the highest form of healing anyone can ever experience. To me, it's just an extra blessing when God, an angel, or an ascended master decides to come through a reading or a healing to deliver a message. Sometimes, you just never know who will come through! I am always humbled when I do this work, and I am thankful for every opportunity.

MY CONVERSATION WITH HEAVEN

It is in this chapter I will talk a bit about God, as I think it's important within these pages. What is your faith? It's a question I never get — really, I don't! Since I talk to the dead, some people believe that I am going straight to Hell! Or perhaps I know something that they are too fearful to really trust. Or perhaps they don't think anything about it at all, and I like that; we are all individuals, and I encourage people to ask themselves what they believe.

Most people who see me believe in a higher power of some sort. My life has been so full of experiences that keep me guessing and trying to understand life and the Afterlife. One night in a dream, I was brought into a room with my guide. I was astral-travelling again.

I remember being escorted down a hall that looked like a courtroom. Curious, I looked at my guide and asked again, "Why am I here?" He gently spoke. "Don't worry. We will be out of here soon, and everything will be okay." The doors opened, and it was a courtroom, looking just like the courtrooms we see on TV. Then I was sitting at a huge table; it was long and oval shaped. Everything around the table seemed to be a whitish colour. I couldn't see anything else in the room or on the walls. The individuals surrounding the table were looking at sheets of paper with their heads down, and they seemed to be wearing long gowns like a judge wears; they were of a light colour. I felt safe with my guide, yet I was worried I had done something wrong. I stood there feeling ready yet not knowing why I felt this way.

My attention was brought to a man who was sitting at the head of the table. He seemed to be the leader or someone of high superiority, and I felt like I didn't want to move, even in the slightest. There was no doubt in my mind — this man was a man of authority who held much power over me! He had pure white hair. It was cut short, and it was thick. He wore a suit, which looked kind of grayish. He had a stern yet gentle look on his face. I wasn't afraid; my guide Joe was with me, and the man felt very comfortable to be around. I knew him from somewhere yet from nowhere. Joe began to speak. I remember him saying, "We must apologize for her actions, for she did not know."

The man with the white hair replied very loudly, "Why did she not know?"

"She forgot. They all seem to forget when they arrive, and it takes years for each of them to remember." He apologized once again and said, "We are all working with her so she will remember and she will be able to deliver the messages."

I was standing there pretty much dazed and confused about the whole thing and about this particular conversation! After they stopped talking, I began to move towards this man with gray hair who was sitting at the end of this oval table, and I wasn't walking myself; with his eyes, he brought my body towards him, and this is exactly what he said: "My dear child, I know it is difficult at times to remember who you are, but you must try. I know the angelic energies are important and help every soul on this planet, and you must continue with this growth. However, the most important angelic energy, the holiest source of all, is God. Please don't forget. It is God and God only who is the main Creator; others are leaders and mentors."

As I woke up from this dream or travel, I felt little confused, a bit perplexed, and worried. Yet somehow I knew, deep in my soul, he was right! And I knew it all along.

Even though I bring Archangel Michael into all of my readings and I bring deceased loved ones through for readings, healings, and my life coaching, God is always the one I pray to. I really knew deep down inside he was the one I was answering to in my life.

Based on the information I have received from my guides and angels and the other side, I have learned we are all here to connect with ourselves and God himself. Each one of us is here to learn, grow, and move forward with our soul's growth.

I am a strong believer that my life may not have turned out as well today, or I may not be here on this planet, if I did not have the help from God and the angels. I needed to help myself first, but their guidance was reassuring and helpful on all occasions.

PAST LIVES

My guides have explained to me that when we pass over, we can remain in Heaven until all of our loved ones have passed over into the light. This is why we can contact the dead. At death, your guides and angels guide you into the light; you then are greeted by all of your loved ones. You may have never known your great-grandmother, but if she hasn't reincarnated yet, you can be well assured she will be there to say hello.

When it is time to reincarnate, you and your guides, angels, and God are all together, deciding what it is you need to learn for your soul's next evolution. Healing and knowledge is gained in Heaven; however, your real soul lessons are done through living on earth.

Earlier in the book, I mentioned that I have had many past lives and that my soul may have been around for hundreds, if not thousands, of years, learning and experiencing everything the world had to offer.

I have been a nun in a previous life; this may in fact be why I had a desire to be one when I was younger. I have lived within the Lemurian age, in the Atlantean era and in Egyptian times (as an Egyptian goddess, of course). I lived in the time of Jesus and followed him and his teachings. I lived in the Medieval and Middle Ages, and I was burned at the cross for knowing too much about remedies that could help people at that time. I have also had a past life with my husband, and we had a daughter together who died very young, and another past life with one of my sons, where he was my brother.

Past lives can be very interesting indeed, when and if the need arises to investigate them. I believe past lives can hold the key to healing a present life by helping you identify who you were before, why you are where you are today, and why you are experiencing what you are experiencing in your current life. It's not for everyone, though. You need to have an open mind and heart to really receive benefit from this healing journey.

When we move through the journey of embracing and healing the self, we get in touch with our true identities — our true selves. However, to get to the center core within each of us, we have to peel back the layers of the emotional body; this can be painful. It's a little like peeling an onion; one layer at a time brings tears, but the closer we get to the middle, the easier it gets. In essence when we get to the core of the doorway of the soul, we become more empowered, healed, a light turns on; we shift the connection from the lower self to the higher self. Past life healing can help with this.

I work on the premise that all our past lives sit within our energy field, or the soul. Whichever past life needs to be healed first will be the first area of contact. It's best not to go over three past lives within one sitting if you have lived some difficult lives in the past.

We can actually go in and heal the past life by taking some specific steps when you are in a relaxed state. When you enter into a past life healing, you are always aware of what is going on, and you are never guided into anything dangerous or put through something you don't want to experience or see. Remember, your mind is very powerful, and it will not hurt you when you set the proper intentions.

Since I have been providing past life healings, I am amazed at how many people actually suffer from abandonment issues and from unresolved grief in a past life. When we look at their current lives today, we can see some very familiar patterns that may have also been brought forward from a past life. In essence, this validates to me that we do in fact carry soul lessons within our souls. If a soul was unable to heal and grow in a previous life, it is mirrored within a current life to help a person move forward, to help the soul grow.

We need to see why we have experienced what we have experienced. Your soul chose to reincarnate within this lifetime for a reason. What's the reason? This knowledge is key for your growth, for your awakening. Every soul is as unique as every fingerprint is, so it's imperative that you learn from your life lessons and move forward. Don't leave any stone unturned.

As I have mentioned earlier, you are not meant to stay with your heartaches or be unable to move or grow from your difficult situations. Your soul requires movement, and a past life healing can be a part of your healing. I know my past life healing and regression gave me a tremendous amount of clarity and healing for my own soul's journey.

SOUL HEALING

One of the most amazing experiences I have had when doing mediumship readings is how polite and forgiving spirits are. This knowledge has helped me with my own healing. For years I worried my parents were mad at me from the spirit world for the mistakes I made earlier in my life. It was such a relief when I found out later that this was never the case.

In fact, they were trying very hard to help me from the Afterlife.

Like I have said before, it is in Heaven where our loved ones understand and learn about healing and acceptance after they have passed. I think it's important to remember that everyone is exactly placed where he or she was meant to be in life and it's up to the person to make the choice to move forward or to stay exactly where he or she is.

One day I was doing a reading for a lady. Her boyfriend had recently passed over from a suicide. I was contacted within three weeks after his passing, and he came through effortlessly. He spoke about his departure and all the moments he had had in his lifetime that caused his girlfriend pain, and he apologized to her for his actions; he needed healing. He asked if she could somehow find it in her heart to forgive him, and she said she could. A lot of crying and healing took place within that hour. I could see and feel how both their energies shifted when this happened; this moment of healing truly was a gift from God.

When a deep healing comes through like this, I just want to sit in prayer and give thanks for my life. This specific lady saw me more than once — most people do. We had three readings throughout the year, and on the third one she already knew she was ready to move on with another relationship and that her previous boyfriend welcomed it; this brought her peace.

Her boyfriend who had passed told me to tell her he was okay that she started dating again, and he said her new boyfriend was a good man! He told me to tell her that it was all okay. He knew she was ready to move forward. Remember, I had no idea she was even in a relationship until the spirit told me. He gave his blessings and once she heard this, she was ready to move on without harbouring any pain or guilt.

Our loved ones want to help prepare our souls for the journey of life, and they can do this from Heaven. Our loved ones in Heaven aren't worried about how much money you're going to make, or are making, or even what kind of a job you have. They want to make sure you are happy and being a good person, period.

I don't necessarily believe I am an expert in life or death, I am always learning. I have learned so much from the Afterlife and realize today that love and forgiving is one of the most important elements of life.

I can tell you for certain, your loved ones really are in a wonderful place, and they can see you every day! I guess we create our own Heaven or Hell.

I have learned from my own past experience that Hell is only created from our fears. In life, we must have Heaven and Hell to create balance; we would not know one without the other. Both are part of the divine plan, and you can live your life in either realm; it's all up to you.

I'm not trying to lecture anyone reading this book; I am trying to allow you to see a different perspective from a person who can communicate with the other side — a person who has endured much pain herself, and a person who took the time to heal and acknowledge the truth of her life purpose and life itself.

If you knew me years ago — essentially what I wrote in the beginning of this book — you would know that I personally struggled with becoming who I am and what my purpose is. Yet my guides, then, told me to move forward. I was helping change people's lives.

I believe from the bottom of my heart that God and my angels gave me hope and guided me towards living a better life. But I needed to listen and make sure I was following the steps that were laid in front of me. It took a lot of courage, believe me.

When I opened my heart to my true self, I had fears and doubt — who wouldn't? I didn't wake up one day and say, "Hey, I want to be a psychic medium." No, Spirit and God led the way on this one. With a series of personal circumstances that happened early in my life, it was pretty hard to accept that something was a little different with me, so I struggled. I struggled with self-doubt and fear. Every time I experienced some type of self-doubt, something miraculous or life-changing would happen.

When I did my first Angel Party (this is what I used to call them), I would get together with a group of people and give 20-minute readings to each. With my first one, I was a little scared.

The location of the party turned out to be one block away from the house I had built with my second husband — the same place where an angel's wings had wrapped around me for comfort and protection. I live in a city where about a million people live. Imagine the odds of this! Even though I learned to let go and embrace my new life, I certainly didn't visit the neighborhood. So I really had to remind myself not to worry but to believe and trust in God, and I would do fine. That night I helped many people experience life-altering events and healing; I was full of the joy of reuniting loved ones. What could be better? So as the years went along, I continued with group readings. However, Spirit was calling me to once again step out of my comfort zone. I was to start reaching a larger audience. Even though I like talking, I, too, can get nervous in front of crowds. So I said in prayer, "Okay I will do this, but I will start small."

I began advertising my "messages from the Afterlife." I provided random readings to larger groups of people. When I had my first registration, I didn't know where the group was going to meet until one week prior. Feeling comfortable with the city I lived in, I waited until the day before to Google the location for directions. To my astonishment, it was one block away from where I had lived with my first husband, when I was really young! Coincidence? I think not, as I don't believe in coincidences. No, there was a message here, and I was going to hear it no matter what.

I was early for the appointment, so I stopped at a corner store, and right across from me was the old house. No, this was not planned. As I looked around, I chuckled to myself and thought, *Okay, what's the message?* I went in and started looking for some answers. I thought, *What am I afraid of?* In the worst-case scenario, someone (a spirit) wouldn't come through for someone (in our world). I mean, I knew that someone would show up for a couple of them because Spirit always shows up. So why was I afraid? Then I heard that voice from my guide, a voice I knew was not my own. I heard, "Look how far you have come." In an instant, I wanted to cry, and I was reminded how far I really had come from that little girl who felt worthless, who had low self-esteem, who was scared of her abilities, and who was afraid everyone would think she was crazy. Spirit sent me a message about what I needed to be reminded of. I had grown into a person who had shared tons of verifiable messages from Spirit, and I was a survivor. So I put my smile on and drove to my appointment.

This being my first time with a large group, I experienced something I hadn't felt in a very long time. When I finished with my beginning prayer, all of a sudden Spirit took over! At times I felt out of my body. I was in a light trance (mediumship phase); completely aware of what was going on and in full control, I opened my mouth, and all information came through! When I was finished, I felt like I had been given this amazing jolt of energy. I felt uplifted, inspired, and ready for whatever was to come my way.

You see, when you get ideas of places you want to go, companies you want to create, or a life you want to live, these are desires of the soul. You can make things work, if you want to. You will get tested time and time again. It's part of the soul's growth and part of life, so when life gets tough or you become overpowered by FEAR, you have to brush yourself off and get up again. Know that success and happiness are just around the corner. You wouldn't have such deep desires to live your life better if you were not able to bring any of those desires to life.

My husband and I went for a walk one morning, something I do regularly, and we spoke about the freedom of self-esteem and knowledge and how it has benefited my journey.

I said to him that more than anything, this journey has made me realize it's okay to be me. I am a woman who lives within her power, who knows that she has a higher calling and is living it. When I first ventured into opening my business, my husband asked me, "Are you ready for this?"

"Ready for what?" I asked.

"Well", he said, "you're going to be met with some opposition. Not everyone believes in this kind of work."

I looked at him and said, "I do!" And I always stand on my word. *And so the journey continues ...*

I pray that you see love inside you and all around you daily. I pray that love never leaves you and you have the faith and courage to make it through every twist and turn that comes your way. I pray that you keep kindness in your heart and remember God and the soul will always show you the way! Love you! —Marnie Hill

NOTES:

NOTES:

NOTES:

Lightning Source UK Ltd.
Milton Keynes UK
UKHW011253301219
356115UK00006B/1812/P